The History of the
Vietnam
War
W9-CBL-079

Exeter Books

NEW YORK

A Bison Book

The History of the Vietnam War

Douglas Welsh

Published in USA 1984
by Exeter Books
Distributed by Bookthrift
Exeter is a trademark of Simon & Schuster
Bookthrift is a registered trademark of Simon & Schuster
New York, New York

ISBN 0-671-06814-8

Printed in Hong Kong

Reprinted 1984

Contents

Foreword

This book is an expression of the events of the Vietnam conflict as seen through the eyes of one who is not only a military historian but was a combat advisor in Vietnam. It is not intended to be an extensive compilation of military and political facts, but rather a general view of what in my opinion were key factors in the course and final outcome of the Vietnam war.

Unlike the subjects of other military histories, Vietnam has resulted in few ultimate and accepted findings. In essence Vietnam is a conglomeration of loose ends. Yet the very nature of the indecisiveness and the quantity of unknowns speaks for itself. Even when refering to Vietnam a question of semantics is posed. Random House Dictionary's primary definition of 'Conflict' is 'to come into collision or disagreement: be at variance or in opposition; clash'. That same source defines 'war': as 'a major armed conflict between nations or between organized parties within a state'. It served the interest of politicians of the highest rank to contain Vietnam in the guise of the term 'conflict', but there can be no question for those who fought and died in Vietnam. It was war.

The books on Vietnam have dealt with the political, economic, and military aspects of the war, as well as the destruction, death, agony and remorse suffered by those who were involved. Yet the majority of Americans have still to understand precisely how and why the United States involvement in Vietnam began and escalated. The cause of wars can be attributed to many factors, principal of which are nationalistic fervor, economic gains, power struggles and military

ventures. It is the question of the courses of the US involvement that can hopefully be answered. As an historian I will attempt to reveal all possible aspects of that question as well as others related to the Vietnam conflict. As a combat veteran my attempt to do so may at times show a different perspective and an occasional lapse from total objectivity.

Below: UH-1D 'Huey' helicopters lift off after unloading members of the 1st ARVN Division in the A Shau Valley. The Huey was the most widely used transport helicopter in Vietnam.

The Unknown War

Most Americans of the late 1950s and 1960s had not heard of Vietnam. A few people knew that it was in the Far East or Southeast Asia. An even smaller number was able to make an intelligent guess about the prevailing conditions there. As a boy I remember leafing through a thin book and looking at the inserted photographs of a naval doctor and an oriental people. When questioned, my older sister told me that it was about the 'poor suffering people' in a place called Vietnam and the work that a Doctor Dooley was performing.

The incident took place in 1960 when I was 10 years old. A dynamic new president, John F Kennedy, was uniting the nation's hopes with his charismatic appeal. A new dawn, a new greatness, a new direction could be sensed during that time. The feeling of belonging to the greatest nation of the world, one that was powerful and could do no wrong was very much a part of the times. Great adventures were in store for my generation. Little did we know then just what kind of adventures they would be or how the country of Dr Dooley's *Deliver Us From Evil* would affect our lives. The United States was riding a wave of optimism and self-confidence which would be violently shaken in the very near future.

Below: men of the 1st Cavalry Division (Airmobile) advance toward Viet Cong positions near Bong Son early in 1966.

Opposite: a US Army sergeant from the 1st Infantry Division wades through a jungle stream during a search-and-destroy operation.

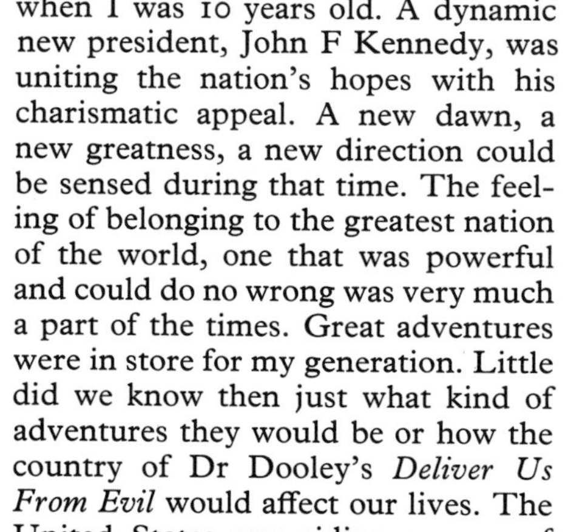

Vietnam shook this mood of self-confidence. Accusations and blame have been shifted from one segment of the nation to another. One group claims to have been betrayed. Another insists that the generation that fought in Vietnam did not have the guts to win a war. Others blamed Congress and the President. For some the issue was stopping Communism, for others it was seen as a return to Imperialism. There remain to the present strong and conflicting opinions about Vietnam, but few understand the war any more clearly than they did back in the early 1960s.

The first topic must therefore be how the situation in Vietnam developed and what led to American involvement. A desire for self-determination was emerging in Vietnam during the early 1950s as it had for virtually all the people who were part of the old colonial empires. Discontent had been present and the situation created by World War II sped the process. World War II caused a disruption of the European dominance and revitalized the idea of self-rule. The Japanese tried desperately to unite most of the peoples of Asia under the slogan of 'Asia for the Asiatics.' Although the attempt failed miserably from the Japanese viewpoint, it gave a means of expression to those who believed that it was time to become the masters of their own destiny. Throughout the world peoples who were still part of the massive colonial empires had reached the stage where they wanted to be rid of European domination. The Japanese gave a conclusive demonstration to the people of Southeast Asia that the Europeans could be beaten militarily by an Asian army. Asian people had reached the crucial period of their history when they were ready for an attempt at self-determination, and they had also seen the Europeans in defeat.

After World War II the victors prepared to resume control of Japanese-occupied colonies. France's Indochina colony was restored with little regard for the aspirations of a nationalistic movement among the people. But the people had fought the Japanese during the war not with the idea of returning the French to power, but to eliminate another Imperialistic master, Japan. The strongest element in the nationalist movement during that era in Vietnam was led by a man who had adopted the name Ho Chi Minh. As early as 1941 his Indochinese Communist Party called for the liberation of Vietnam from French

domination. Its political and military organization was the Viet Minh.

Throughout World War II the Viet Minh fought bitterly against the Japanese, with the aim of establishing an independent republic in Indochina. The Japanese sought to appease the nationalistic movement, without success, by promising independence under Japan's protection. A government had been established by the Japanese under Emperor Bao Dai which actually did more to antagonize the feelings of those in the nationalist movement. Although the puppet government remained in power throughout the war it never achieved any of the aims the Japanese had intended.

After the war the French returned. The major issues confronting them were rooted in the northern sectors of the country where the Viet Minh were especially active in their demands for self-determination. In the south the Viet Minh were not as strong. The people who lived in the region between Hue and Saigon seemed to consider colonial rule inevitable, whether it be by the Japanese or the French, and they were easily brought back into line by the French. However, in September 1945 the Democratic Republic of Viet Nam was proclaimed by Ho Chi Minh as he called for the abdication of Bao Dai and the right to self-determination for the Vietnamese people. The declaration of independence was drawn up along the same lines as the United States Declaration of Independence of 1776 and called for the same basic rights and freedoms as that document, in the hope that the Americans would rally to support the cause of Vietnamese independence. It even went so far as to begin, 'All men are created equal and they are endowed by their Creator with certain inalienable rights. And among these are Life, Liberty, and the Pursuit of Happiness.'

The elections which followed were overwhelmingly in favor of the Viet Minh position, which won more than 400 seats in the National Assembly. Ho Chi Minh was proclaimed president of the new republic. He demanded the immediate withdrawal of the French and complete independence for the former colony. Ho Chi Minh's security at the time the demands were being made was the support and aid he was receiving from two major sources. The first was the Communist Chinese who had helped to train the Viet Minh and had fought side by side with them against the Japanese. American OSS Teams were Ho Chi Minh's other allies and they had been advising him and his military commander, Vo Nguyen Giap, in the previous struggle with the Japanese. During World War II the Americans supported the Communist factions aiding the Viet Minh as they had proven themselves to be the most effective fighting force against the Japanese. In fact many in the Intelligence community considered Ho

Left: Viet Minh troops charge French infantrymen across a flooded paddy field.
Top: French troops comb through a jungle thicket in search of Viet Minh snipers during Operation Lorraine in January 1953.
Above: Nguyen Xuan Thuy addresses the World Council of Peace at Vienna on the Vietnamese problem in November 1953.

Above : a map of Vietnam at the time of the French withdrawl in 1954. The partition between North and South was on the 17th Parallel.

Above right : troopers of the 101st Airborne Division beat off a Viet Cong attack during Operation Hawthorne in mid-1966.
Right : US troops occupy trenches dug by the Viet Cong in Kontum Province during Operation Hawthorne.
Left : men of Charlie Company, 2nd Battalion, 7th Cavalry Regiment advance on a VC bunker.

Chi Minh's organization to be the only stable leadership in the region.

Owing to the Chinese and OSS influence the French found it extremely difficult to oppose the Viet Minh. However, by late 1945 the OSS Teams were finally withdrawn, leaving the doorway open for the French. The following year the French agreed to recognize the Republic, with the stipulation that it would remain part of France. The French also agreed that, if at some point in the future it became obvious that the people throughout the country wished to unite under Ho Chi Minh's rule, a referendum would be held to confirm their desires.

In both Hue and Paris talks continued in an effort to negotiate a working agreement between the French and the Viet Minh. Those negotiations finally broke down in December 1945 owing to the unwillingness of either party to concede or compromise. Subsequently armed confrontation erupted between the Viet Minh, newly dubbed the National Front, and French troops. It was at that point that the country of Vietnam made its initial division. Ho Chi Minh was most firmly established in the northern regions and he took his government and his followers and relocated in Hanoi. The French, whose power base was in the southern region, set up their colonial government in Saigon.

From 1946–53 French and allied Vietnamese units fought against the Viet Minh. The war primarily consisted of guerrilla actions which gave

neither faction a clear upper hand, although the attrition factor and the length of the conflict seemed to weigh heavily against the French. This could be attributed to the French military policy, which was not appropriate to the new style of warfare being waged. Although they made desperate attempts to search out and bring the Viet Minh to grips it was virtually impossible. The Viet Minh retained the choice of whether to fight or melt away into the mountains and jungles.

Ho Chi Minh knew that it was impossible for the French and the colonial Vietnamese troops to hold all locations simultaneously or even to deny the Viet Minh their traditional power bases. The French strategy was therefore simple: to hold the main populated areas and major lines of communication, biding their time and hoping to draw the guerrillas into a major action which would destroy their effectiveness. By adopting that policy they relinquished any hope of holding the countryside, or retaining the loyalty of the peasants. Ho Chi Minh also waited, primarily in the hope that the French government and people would grow tired of the conflict, the casualties and the futility of the situation and relinquish their claims in Indochina. This wearing down process would take time and General Giap and other members of Ho Chi Minh's command were eager for the chance to catch the French in a poor position where a victory could be quickly won without jeopardizing the revolution. Such a victory would speed the process to eliminate colonial rule.

Between 1946 and 1953 Viet Minh strength and numbers had doubled. Although the French attempted to play down the guerrillas the situation was at last becoming critical. In 1953 the French government appointed General Henri Navarre as the new overall commander of French forces in Indochina. He decided on a new strategy. He would set a trap and bait it with a large French force in an area which was considered a power base of the guerrillas. Once he goaded the Viet Minh into battle, Navarre would apply 'French military superiority' to destroy the guerrillas once and for all. The site that was finally chosen lay in a small valley in northwestern Vietnam, approximately 25 miles from the Laotian border, 75 miles from China, and 150 miles west of Hanoi. The bait was a large airborne assault force which was to secure the valley and deserted airfield, then establish a fortification around that airfield. When the guerrillas attacked the French defenders would destroy them.

This operation resulted in one of the greatest battles of the post-World War II era, Dien Bien Phu. The real significance of the battle lies in its cause, and effects its outcome would produce. The French were defeated at Dien Bien Phu for several primary reasons. First and most important, Navarre and his generals unquestionably underestimated their guerrilla opponents' determined fighting capability and willingness to attempt the seemingly impossible. On that basis the French handled the operation poorly from the start. The fortifications at Dien Bien Phu which the French erected fell far short of what

Below : Viet Minh troops were supplied by bicycle during the buildup before the Battle of Dien Bien Phu. The same means of supply was also used along the Ho Chi Minh Trail in the war against the South Vietnamese and Americans.
Right : the Viet Minh examine a pile of rifles captured from the French.
Below right : the North Vietnamese leader Ho Chi Minh poses with a group of youthful supporters.

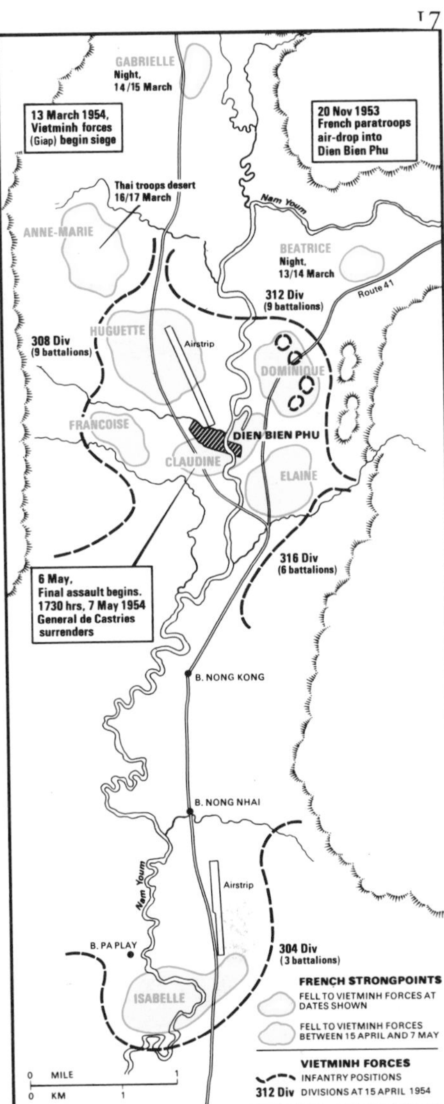
GABRIELLE
Night,
14/15 March
13 March 1954,
Vietminh forces
(Giap) begin siege
20 Nov 1953
French paratroops
air-drop into
Dien Bien Phu
Thai troops desert
16/17 March
Nam Youm
ANNE-MARIE
BEATRICE
Night,
13/14 March
312 Div
(9 battalions)
Route 41
HUGUETTE
308 Div
(9 battalions)
Airstrip
DOMINIQUE
FRANCOISE
DIEN BIEN PHU
CLAUDINE
ELAINE
316 Div
(6 battalions)
6 May,
Final assault begins.
1730 hrs, 7 May 1954
General de Castries
surrenders
B. NONG KONG
B. NONG NHAI
Nam Youm
Airstrip
B. PA PLAY
304 Div
(3 battalions)
ISABELLE
FRENCH STRONGPOINTS
FELL TO VIETMINH FORCES AT DATES SHOWN
FELL TO VIETMINH FORCES BETWEEN 15 APRIL AND 7 MAY
VIETMINH FORCES
INFANTRY POSITIONS
312 Div DIVISIONS AT 15 APRIL 1954
0 MILE 1
0 KM 1

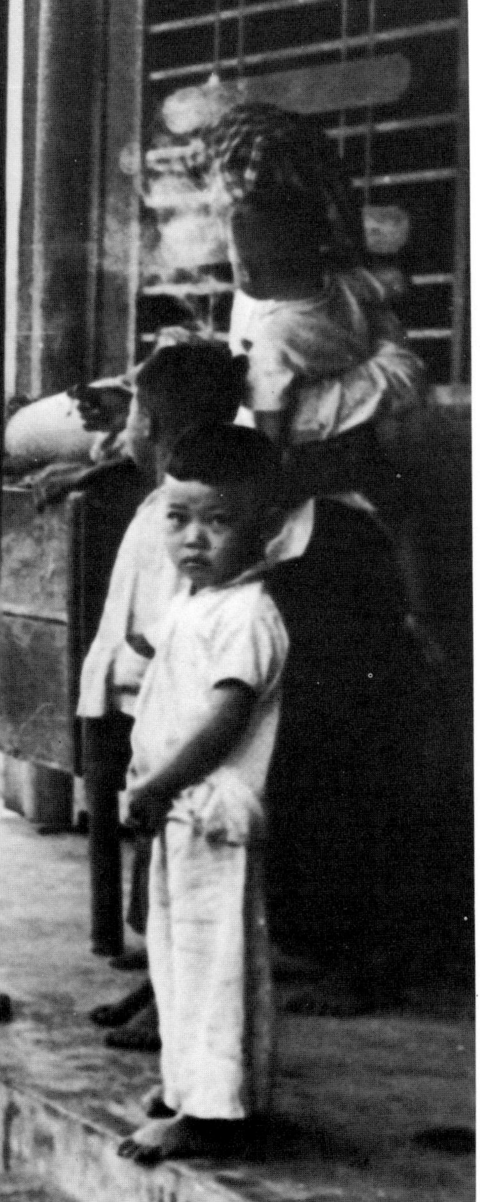

Above far left: exultant Viet Minh troops pose on the wreck of a French air force Douglas C-47 transport aircraft.
Left: a South Vietnamese army patrol moves into a hamlet in search of Viet Cong guerrillas.

Above left: South Vietnamese soldiers guard a Viet Cong prisoner, who was captured in a raid at Camau in the Mekong Delta in 1962.
Above: French wounded are tended after an attack on a strongpoint at Dien Bien Phu in 1954.

was required. They were outmanned, outgunned and outmaneuvered. Although the bravery of the defenders at Dien Bien Phu, especially the paratroopers of the Foreign Legion whose heroics were made legendary, cannot be questioned, they could not save the situation.

The French had a great deal of confidence in the propaganda of their own military and political endeavors which would ultimately backfire both during and after their loss at Dien Bien Phu. They were preaching superiority and minimizing the guerrilla threat. Therefore when the French were defeated at Dien Bien Phu it caused a shock wave to run through the French society and government, destroying the will to continue the war.

Dien Bien Phu was a turning point for the Viet Minh and the new Republic and on 20 July 1954, talks which were being held in Geneva, Switzerland, between the two main parties produced an agreement. The Geneva Agreement was a working plan for the smooth transition of power from the French government to the Vietnamese, ending colonial rule in Vietnam. Fundamentally the agreement divided Indochina into four parts, creating the countries now known as Laos, Cambodia and Vietnam. Further, Vietnam was divided along the seventeenth parallel with the Viet Minh under Ho Chi Minh ruling the North and the French helping to establish a Vietnamese government in the South. The French remained because they would not sign an agreement and acquiesce to terms which gave full control to the Viet Minh and left France completely out of the Indochina picture. Under the terms of the agreement, the division of Vietnam was to last for two years, after which elections were to be held to determine whether the divided country wished to be reunified.

The two states had completely different ideological bases. The North, under the leadership of Ho Chi Minh, was a strong communist regime which had brought about the fall of the French and viewed itself as the rightful government of not only Vietnam but all of what had been French Indochina. The South was an anti-Communist regime supported by the French and headed by Emperor Bao Dai. The division of Vietnam resulted in a basic economic problem. The northern region had traditionally been the industrial center, having the natural resources with which to support its industries. The southern

French troops watch the evacuation of wounded comrades from Dien Bien Phu by Sikorsky H-19 helicopter.

regions, particularly the Mekong Delta, had been traditionally agricultural. It became evident that, if Vietnam was not to be united, both factions would have to look elsewhere to meet these deficiencies.

Also during those two years a major shift in population occurred. The large Catholic population of the North feared that the new Communist regime would retaliate against them for their support of the French. Approximately 85 percent of the 900,000 Catholics began a great exodus to the South. In the South it was estimated that 100,000 Viet Minh 'stationed' throughout the region began their own exodus northward – in this case not out of fear but by order of the Hanoi government – who ordered the move to consolidate the Viet Minh's strength. Most of these former guerrillas did indeed move north, but at least 5000 of their ranks remained behind as cadre for future operations if the French failed to live up to their bargain to allow the people to determine their own fate and the question of reunification.

Ho Chi Minh took the vote issue entirely for granted as he turned all of his efforts toward establishing his government in the North and solving the economic and social problems which were facing him. He was confident that he would win the elections but he did not overlook the possibility that the South would be aided in its own establishment by outside influence, particularly the United States. What Ho Chi Minh did seem to overlook was that the Geneva Agreement was primarily between two parties: himself, representing the Viet Minh, and the French. Of those two parties, he was the only participant left in Vietnam by 1956. Neither the South Vietnamese government nor the

United States signed the agreement and as such felt they had no reason to abide by it. Thus, grounds were conveniently given for the cancellation of the elections by the American supported Premier of South Vietnam, Ngo Dinh Diem.

The Geneva Agreement comprised a great many articles intended to establish order and prevent the future eruption of armed conflict in Southeast Asia. Military limitations were of primary concern and every effort was made to insure that alliances formed by the two principal factions within the country of Vietnam did not interfere with the balance of power as it then existed.

An International Commission, whose members were India, Poland, and Canada, was established to oversee

Left: two Viet Cong prisoners are escorted by ARVN infantrymen. Below: an ARVN soldier examines a cache of Viet Cong propaganda, which was discovered during an operation in the Mekong Delta. Below right: a guard of honor stands knee deep in water while waiting for President Diem's arrival.

the agreement. Unfortunately that commission lacked the will or the ability to influence events. The failure of the Commission opened the doors for new powers to take the place of those which would soon fade from the scene. Just as Diem would gradually increase his power sphere to replace the self-exiled Bao Dai, so the United States would begin, quietly at first, to assume the support role vacated by the French.

The groundwork had been laid for the seeds of conflict in Vietnam, but a broader picture must be viewed to understand fully the scope of the situation that evolved. When the Geneva Agreement divided North and South along the seventeenth parallel, it created Laos and Cambodia. Cambodia can briefly be described as a country which tried to play all sides against one another. It was a declared neutral, yet made no effort to protect its borders from outside influence. It was also the only state involved which refused to sign the Geneva Agreement of 1954 and it was led primarily by one man, Prince Norodom Sihanouk. From 1941–70 he held numerous positions, including king, political leader, and head of state. Although the war would be briefly led into Cambodia in later years, in the early days it was Laos that was most involved.

The head of the Laotian government, Prince Souvanna Phouma, tried to fashion a neutralist coalition government of both pro-Western and pro-Communist supporters. The Communist support faction was known as the Pathet Lao which had Prince Souvanna Phouma's half-brother, Prince Souphanouvong, as its leading figure. The pro-Western faction was led by Prince Boun Oum. Boun Oum also had the support of the 25,000-man Royal Laotian Army, which was supported militarily and funded by the United States Government.

In those early days both factions tried desperately to gain an advantage in the government. In the 1958 elections Prince Souphanouvong's party received the greatest number of votes and the United States saw its position begin to deteriorate. The United States put pressure on Souvanna Phouma to resign his position in favor of an American backed successor, Phoui Sananikone, who would continue the neutralist policy and offset the gains of Souphanouvong's party in the coalition.

Early in 1959 the conflict between the American-backed Phoui Sananikone and the pro-Communist party led to Souphanouvong's arrest and a swing toward the West. That swing included members of the factions' military forces, who were being united by the neutralist government into the Royal Laotian Army. However, on hearing of Souphanouvong's arrest, a Pathet Lao battalion scheduled for integration into the army fled to the North Vietnamese border and began conducting guerrilla actions against the Laotian government. Less than one year later Prince Souphanouvong managed to escape and joined the Communist forces in the north.

The country of Laos had definitely shifted toward the West, yet many Laotians felt that this was a mistake and that the neutralist policy should be maintained. A young captain, Kong Le, who commanded the elite paratroop battalion of the Royal Laotian Army, seized the Laotian capital, Vientiane. He accused Phoui Sananikone's government of being a puppet-slave of the United States and the United States of trying to establish a colonial sphere of influence over the country. He demanded the reestablishment of Souvanna Phouma's

Below: a South Vietnamese Air Force Douglas A-1 Skyraider pulls away from an attack on Diem's palace in May 1962. The president survived the attack unscathed.
Right: Secretary of Defense Robert McNamara (right) pictured with General Lyman Lemnitzer, Chairman of the Joint Chiefs of Staff, inspects an American advisory unit in Vietnam on 9 May 1962.
Below right: tanks move in on the presidential palace in Saigon after the South Vietnamese air attack.

neutralist policies in the Laotian government.

Once again the tide turned and the neutralist faction was in command with Souvanna Phouma forming the new government. His government, much to the embarrassment of the United States, received support from France and the United Kingdom as well as from the Soviet Union and other Communist nations. It was only the United States and Thailand who supported the right-wing regimes of Boun Oum and Phoumi Nosavan, who had replaced Prince Phoui Sananikone.

The Soviet Union began to take an active role in flying supplies from North Vietnam to Kong Le's forces, who were being opposed by the United States supported Royal Army. The aim of the Royal Laotian Army had been openly announced to support the pro-American faction and depose the neutralist regime. When the Royal Army and Kong Le's forces finally met at Vientiane the battle was a massive artillery duel, the main

Left: a US Army advisor demonstrates grenade-throwing techniques to a member of the South Vietnamese Self Defense Corps at Tan Hiep. Below: a wounded Vietnamese villager waits for medical attention. He was caught in crossfire during a fight between the VC and government forces. Right: a Vietnamese infantryman has secured his next meal during a drive against the Viet Cong.

accomplishment of which was the near destruction of the capital and the killing or wounding of more than 1500 civilians, with little or no damage done to either military force. However, Kong Le knew that he could not hold out against the weight of his opponent and retreated to an area in north-central Laos known as the Plain of Jars. Phoumi Nosavan then took control of the government but failed to press his advantage and destroy Kong Le's forces. Those forces would eventually link with the Pathet Lao in the north.

The balance of power remained relatively even. The American government pumped more arms and military aid, including aircraft and US Army Special Forces Advisors into Laos, while the Soviet Union continued to send arms, vehicles, and antiaircraft weapons in support of Pathet Lao and other anti-American elements. North Vietnam responded to the Special Forces Advisors participation by sending North Vietnamese Army (NVA) cadres to train the Communist troops of the Pathet Lao.

The Soviet Union, North Vietnam, and the United States realized that the only way left to break the deadlock would be the actual commitment of combat troops to support their particular factions. Yet no one wanted war in Laos. The United States had several problems. Laos was a landlocked country which would be virtually impossible to supply with troops and equipment once a state of war existed. Although a slight advantage had been gained, the Royal Laotian Army continued to make a poor showing on the battlefield and it was felt that the Laotians did not have the heart to fight in a full-scale war. Furthermore America could find no support from its Western allies. The strategic reserves of the United States were already committed primarily in support of Europe and many felt that a Southeast Asia war would stretch the United States' military to a breaking point. The Soviet government of Nikita Khrushchev did not want such a war for almost the same reasons, except that it found the Pathet Lao soldier much more competent than his Royal Army counterpart.

So the conflict could serve no true purpose for the Soviet Union or the United States. The Pathet Lao were satisfied with biding their time. Sooner or later they were certain that the West would lose interest. Of those who were interested in the situation, North Vietnam continued to be concerned about the Ho Chi Minh Trail, their supply line that ran through Laos and Cambodia to support the guerrilla activities in the South. China, another interested party, was concerned only with the safeguarding of its borders.

In May 1961 meetings which were being held in Geneva produced an agreement which recognized Laos as a neutral, independent country. The Laotian Accords contained four principal articles: the declaration of the neutrality of Laos; all nations outside Laos would respect the sovereignty of Laos and refrain from interfering in its internal affairs; aid to Laos could not include the setting up of bases within the country, nor military alliances with any faction; the establishment of a government in which Prince Souvanna Phouma would become head of the government, Prince Souphanouvong would be considered second in command, and Phoumi Nosavan would be responsible for all financial affairs. Although the article which prohibited the military interference and aid was one that looked well on paper, it was not a point that the involved parties were willing to commit themselves to unequivocally.

No sooner had the negotiations been finalized than Phoumi Nosavan's faction struck out on its own, refusing to cooperate with the new coalition cabinet. As he was the head of the pro-American faction Phoumi Nosovan assumed that the United States would support him in any endeavor and he massed troops of the Royal Army on the Chinese border. On 6 May 1962, after many probing attacks, North Vietnamese and Pathet Lao forces

defeated Phoumi Nosavan's army. This not only humiliated Phoumi Nosavan but paved the way for the establishment of a coalition government of neutralists, Communists and right-wing elements. For the most part the civil war in Laos was over, but both the North Vietnamese and Americans would continue to use that country's unrest as a pawn in the larger struggle in Vietnam.

John F Kennedy, who had become President of the United States in 1960, was having many problems with the deteriorating situation in Southeast Asia. Not only did the problems in Laos plague him, but Kennedy was receiving mounting pressure from Congress not to get the United States involved in any military confrontation. His disastrous Bay of Pigs Invasion in Cuba had deeply shaken his self-confidence. He could ill afford another political embarrassment in his foreign policy such as Laos might bring him. With the Laotian Accords it was evident that he must give up the Laotian affair. Instead he would shift support entirely behind Diem's regime in South Vietnam to maintain the anti-Communist position in that part of Indochina.

As Kennedy shifted the focus of attention to South Vietnam, he was becoming involved at a most unstable time. More than 600 incidents per month were attributed to the Communist insurgents. More than 75 percent of the country was thought to be under Communist control and the United States Ambassador to South Vietnam, Frederick E Nolting Jr, filed numerous reports indicating widespread dissatisfaction with the Diem Regime. The South Vietnamese government could at best be described as unstable. If in the near future the Communist guerrillas could not be dealt with, there was a high probability that the people would no longer support Diem and his government would collapse.

Ambassador Nolting complained of Diem's unwillingness to cooperate or listen to suggestions made to help bolster his precarious situation. That fact was not helped by the fear in South Vietnam that the United States would simply desert the country as it had deserted Laos. In May 1961 Vice-President Lyndon Johnson was sent on a fact-finding tour of South Vietnam. This visit was intended to accomplish three tasks. First, it was a reaffirmation of United States' support for South Vietnam and Diem.

Above: the Vietnam Junk Force patrolled coastal waters to prevent VC infiltration and arms shipments.
Right: a Junk Force crew moves in on suspected vessels.

Johnson was also to discover exactly what Diem needed to fight the guerrillas and maintain his anti-Communist government. Finally, Johnson was to return to the United States with a first hand analysis of the situation in South Vietnam so that Kennedy could make his own evaluation of the proper course of action.

Vice-President Johnson was given a fairly free hand during his visit to assess the situation and promise Diem any support he required, even to the actual commitment of American troops to Vietnam. However Diem, who was skeptical of Johnson's offer, said he did not want US combat troops. Instead he asked that the United States send more equipment and funds so that he could increase the South Vietnamese army by 30,000 men. Diem also asked for an increase in the Military Assistance and Advisory Group (MAAG) program and for more specialists to increase the training of South Vietnamese troops in support activities such as main-

Right: the defenses of the fortified village of Cu Chi included a deep moat lined with sharpened bamboo stakes and surrounded by barbed wire entanglements.
Below: South Vietnamese local militia are instructed in marksmanship.
Bottom: militiamen prepare for a patrol against the Viet Cong.
Far right: a guard patrols an outpost's fortified perimeter.

tenance and flight training, rather than combat advisors. He further requested the armaments necessary to supply a projected 60,000-man Civil Guard and the advisors to train them. The function of the Civil Guard was to protect the villages in the outlying areas which were controlled and harassed by the Viet Cong guerrilla forces.

Throughout their meetings Diem constantly shifted the blame for all his failures and those of his government onto the fear that the United States would abandon the Vietnamese, as Kennedy had apparently abandoned

the Laotians. He refused to listen to any suggestion which either the Ambassador or Vice-President Johnson tried to make concerning political or social reforms within the country. Although American representatives pressed Diem on the issues of social reforms, Diem and his family power structure firmly believed that he was the leader of South Vietnam by some 'divine right' and that the upper or Mandarin Class must be kept in power, allowing no variation in the social order. Diem's position was completely dependent on that upper class and he was determined not to disturb the status quo.

It was obvious to Johnson, as it was to most American officials in South Vietnam, that unless something was done to raise the morale of the South Vietnamese people the country would swing in favor of the Communists. Kennedy responded to those assessments by sending General Maxwell Taylor to South Vietnam to study the situation and make suggestions on alternatives open to the United States. Taylor's reaction was that the United States should send troops to take an active role alongside the Army of the Republic of Vietnam (ARVN) to end once and for all the doubts about American commitment. He also advocated increased aid to all levels of the military and government agencies in South Vietnam, as Kennedy had known he would. This was necessary if Diem's government was to survive.

Although combat troops were requested, support groups such as air units and Intelligence and reconnaissance units were sent instead. Also, the United States would take charge and reorganize the ARVN under a new American agency, Military Assistance Command Vietnam (MACV). MACV's responsibility would be to centralize South Vietnam's war effort.

The Special Forces Advisors who carried out the operations of MAAG (later MACV), belonged to the United States Army Special Forces organization. This was instituted in the years following World War II and in 1952 10 men were classified as Special Forces personnel. That number would continue to grow as the demand for both support and combat advisors increased in Vietnam.

The original purpose of the organization was the development of a specialized commando unit which could operate behind enemy lines during conventional warfare, particularly in the European Theater. As time went on that perspective changed as the Cold War grew 'hot' in other areas of the globe.

By 1961 American Special Forces comprised highly trained paratroopers who could be air dropped into the most hostile terrain. Special Forces members had an elite status. Many were bilingual. All were extensively trained in a team concept where each man, although having his own specialized purpose, could substitute for any other team member who might be lost during an operation. An air of mystique surrounded these men. Their implied superiority isolated them from the rest of the army and there were many commanders who were openly hostile toward them.

It was not until President Kennedy took a special interest in the team that they found acceptance in the military. He wanted to 'adopt' the Special Forces, which had by then earned the nickname Green Berets from the combat beret they had 'borrowed' from the British World War II commando. Kennedy visualized the Green Beret as a force which could conduct counterinsurgency operations and aid friendly forces of liberation in the Far East and South America. They were in fact to be an extension of his desire to be the protector of democracy throughout the world. The Green Beret, whose motto was 'Free the Oppressed' would become the supertroop to fight Communism anywhere in the world.

As the situation began to develop in Vietnam, Kennedy saw these men as the answer to the Communist movement. What he failed to realise was that the majority of Special Forces personnel were not inspired to fulfill their duties by the situations in Southeast Asia. Most men who volunteered for this elite military group were

Above: an ARVN soldier tears down a Communist propaganda leaflet.
Right: two blindfolded VC suspects await interrogation by an ARVN officer in December 1962.
Below right: a bivouac area abandoned by the VC during an ARVN sweep.
Below: ARVN troops race from their helicopters toward a Viet Cong position in Tay Ninh Province.

eager to fight Communism, but not in Asia or South America. Many of those men were of Eastern European descent and they wanted to return to the countries of their birth to form guerrilla forces and fight for freedom against the Soviet invaders. It is this one aspect of the Green Beret which is seldom noted, that was the key to understanding why, when they were sent to Vietnam, many were so frustrated by the situation they found. They were simply not fighting where they truly wanted to be.

More than 5000 men would ultimately serve under the classification Special Forces/Combat Advisors in Vietnam. Throughout the involvement in Vietnam the majority of these men conducted themselves with a pride and distinction which served to add to their established mystique. Often however, they were segregated from the rest of their countrymen by their peculiar circumstances. Their tendency to remain aloof was viewed with distrust.

That distrust of the Special Forces personnel was also a result of many of the special operations in which they

Top left: a typical VC booby trap, a camouflaged pit with sharpened bamboo stakes in the bottom.
Left: a Vietnamese sergeant of the 7th Division's Intelligence Section questions a suspected Viet Cong.
Top: Captain Tram Tein Khang, the CO of 1st Bn, 7th Division ARVN, briefs two of his officers.
Above: VC propaganda has been scrawled on the wall of a hut at Ly Van Manh.

were involved. One such operation was the Phoenix Program. Although Phoenix was originally designed as an Intelligence-gathering program, it degenerated into a program which helped the South Vietnamese National Police seek out and eliminate Communist agents, officials, and sympathizers. In 1969 for example the United States and South Vietnamese governments set a goal of 'neutralizing' 20,000 Communist agents. Of those arrested it is estimated that less than 20 percent were actually associated with the North Vietnamese Army or Viet Cong. The 'laws' of the Phoenix Program were set at arrest and detention, but at least 30 percent of all suspects arrested were dead before they ever reached detention. The South Vietnamese used the organization, and the sister-program that the Special Forces helped to create in the South Vietnamese Army, known as Luc Luong Dac Biet [LLDB], to settle old debts and maintain the government. It would take the United States Government some time to admit that it had created a Frankenstein's Monster.

Another aspect of the Special Forces which made them different from the mass of soldiers in Vietnam was their association with the Vietnamese people and the ARVN troops. The average ground troops were concerned with fighting the enemy – 'Charlie' – and had the opinion that the South Vietnamese were relatively useless to the war effort. Yet the Special Forces Advisors worked with the South Vietnamese and seemed to like them.

Most of the Special Forces personnel and advisors in Vietnam carried out their war role, only to find themselves ostracized by their own troops and their loyalties divided between their own military and the people they were supposed to be helping.

By mid-1962 Secretary of Defense Robert MacNamara told Kennedy that their new plan was working. Standardization of communications, logistics, and strategy had instilled new confidence into the South Vietnamese army. New tactics had brought the ARVN some successes and with that success a noticeable increase in Viet Cong defections. Although the program was not actually instituted until later in 1964 and 1965, the defection of NVA/VC forces was welcomed and encouraged. The Chieu Hoi (Open Arms) Program was a psychological device which offered amnesty to any NVA/VC soldier who would surrender and transfer his allegiance to the United States and South Vietnam. These defectors were known as Hoi Chanh and many joined the United States forces who dubbed them Kit Carson Scouts.

In spite of the fact that increased military aid had bolstered the Diem regime in 1962 and that the Communist military effort had for a time been thrown off balance, the basic problems still remained. The South Vietnamese people continued to be uncertain in their support for their government. It had been hoped that victory on the battlefield would induce loyalty, but the social reforms Diem had promised were not implemented. Corruption was rampant and the reactions of the South Vietnamese people ranged from anger to apathy, but few were content.

During that period a new strategy was being employed – the fortified hamlet. In some cases civilians had been forcibly removed from their villages and relocated in government-controlled hamlets, allegedly for their own protection. Many of the peasants looked at the walls that were supposed to safeguard them from the VC as little more than prisons. Also, by uprooting the peasant population, more animosity and hatred was being generated, not only against the government, but against the United States which supported it. The reaction to the fortified-hamlet program created a breeding ground for hatred and distrust.

Two factors coincided with the increased hostility of the people toward the Diem government and although they did not seem important, over the course of the war would prove to be decisive. One involved the American media's view of the conflict and the South Vietnamese government. The corruption of Diem's government was coming under close scrutiny. The reaction to the facts uncovered was one of open hostility, especially by the press. The American press, which enjoys a freedom which few countries have

Right and below right: Vietnamese troops of the 21st Division move into a village suspected of hiding VC. Below: soldiers wounded in fighting along the Kinh Xang canal are evacuated to a medical-aid station by boat.

Above: US Army CH-21 helicopters carry ARVN troops into combat. Left: the view from a CH-21 gunner's station as the helicopter approaches its landing zone in Central Vietnam.

ever known, found many of their articles being censored by the South Vietnamese government agencies. Diem regarded the offending correspondents as traitors and Communist sympathizers and tried to expel any newsman who refused to follow the government's set guidelines for reporting the situation. In doing so Diem not only alienated the press, but he turned the newsman into an antagonist which would ultimately lead to Diem's downfall.

The second factor which was of more immediate importance was the Battle of Ap Boc. Vietnamese Intelligence reports in January 1963 revealed that VC guerrillas had a major radio installation in the village of Ap Boc in the Plain of Reeds. From all reports the station had minimal defenses and would be easy prey for the ARVN, who needed a boost in morale. Diem saw the situation as a means of bolstering his image with the press and demonstrating that he

Above CH-21s supported the ARVN in a battle fought on the Plain of Reeds. Right: the gunner of a CH-21 on a casualty-evacuation mission from Tan Son Nhut returns enemy fire.

was getting the job done. He would put the 'lies' being told about him to rest.

Neither Diem nor the army were taking the chance of anything going wrong and causing them embarrassment. A force of one ARVN regiment of infantry with armor support, the elite ARVN Rangers and 51 American advisors was assembled to execute the mission. One of Diem's reasons for using so many advisors was his belief that the American press would be more likely to believe their reports of a 'great victory.' Diem was also aware that the new tactics being employed by the United States in the various programs were not completely understood by his own commanders. The advisors would be there to make certain those tactics worked.

The battle plan was for American helicopters to fly troops in to engage the enemy, while other ARVN forces would encircle the site, cutting off any VC retreat. From the beginning of the

operation everything seemed to go wrong. The Intelligence reports gained by agents in the area were completely inaccurate. The radio station, the primary target, was located there, but its protection was not a mere VC company but the 514th Viet Cong Regular Battalion of more than 400 veteran troops. When the helicopter assault began the VC regulars stood and fought, rather than run like many of the less experienced guerrilla militia had done so often in the past. Also affecting the reaction of the VC troops was the fact that the helicopter was no longer the terrifying weapon it had been when initially used in Vietnam. The guerrillas were already developing tactics to cope with this new weapon.

Five helicopters were lost in that assault. The ARVN troops scattered and once heavy resistance was felt, few of the ARVN officers were willing to commit their troops to the battle. The US advisors attached to the mission tried to encourage the ARVNs to press on with the attack using the new techniques and coordinating the operation to achieve success. The odds

Above left : a typical Montagnard fortified village viewed from a US Army helicopter. The Montagnards were implacable enemies of the Viet Cong. Above : ARVN troops about to be airlifted into the combat area by a CH-21 helicopter in February 1963.

were in the ARVNs favor. They had more men, armored-vehicle support and mobility, but still the commanders, who were not obliged to act upon the advisors' suggestions, held their troops at a safe distance. One advisor became completely frustrated with the armor-support section when its commander refused to move the vehicles forward for fear one might get damaged or destroyed. Throughout the engagement this attitude dominated the ARVN thinking. The Americans finally persuaded the South Vietnamese to make an air drop to close the VC escape route. The airborne troops sent landed nowhere near their target. When artillery support was called for the ARVN batteries managed to maintain a derisory rate of fire of only four rounds per hour. Just before dark a South Vietnamese air strike was made on the enemy units, but it was sadly mismanaged and accidentally bombed friendly troops, causing what the South Vietnamese government later listed as an undetermined number of casualties.

Under cover of darkness the VC forces slipped away and the Battle of Ap Bac ended. The results were 65 ARVN troops killed, more than 100 wounded, and three Americans dead and six wounded, with five helicopters destroyed and 11 others damaged. Viet Cong losses were not known, but all practical evaluations indicated that they were extremely light if not nonexistent. What had gone wrong was really symptomatic of what was wrong with the military situation on the whole. First and foremost the South Vietnamese commanders were hesitant to commit troops to combat,

Left: Montagnard troops practice at the rifle range at the Pleiyit Commando Training Center in 1963. Above left: South Vietnamese regional forces troops attend a training course. Above: Montagnard commandos patrol the hills near their outpost.

fearing retaliations from the government for the casualties they would suffer. An American article had blasted Diem over an incident that had taken place the previous year which reflected the commanders' fears. An ARVN colonel who had won a substantial victory over the guerrillas in his area had sustained moderate casualties during the operation. The colonel had shown great leadership and aggressiveness, which was considered to be generally lacking in the army. Upon hearing of the incident Diem immediately called the colonel, who was due for promotion to brigadier general, to Saigon. Instead of being rewarded, the reports said that the colonel was told that if he sustained one more casualty, not only would his promotion be denied, but he might find himself facing a court martial. This incident broke the officer's spirit and on returning to his unit he refused to engage again the enemy. He received his promotion.

Although Diem denied the incident, its credibility in the press came from the fact that an American colonel, an advisor with the ARVN Fourth Corps, related the story to the press and to his senior officers. Diem's attitude toward casualties stemmed from his belief that his political position could be maintained if the people were not constantly reminded of battlefield casualties and the continuing war. Another reason for his stand on casualties was related to his insecure position. If there were to be no casualties there could be no major battles; and if there was no fighting there could be no heroes. Diem truly feared the rise to favor and power of a military hero from among his generals.

A major problem was being created by the lack of Intelligence information on VC strengths, areas of operation and tactics. The South Vietnamese difficulties and inadequacies would never be completely rectified throughout the entire war in this respect. Even when the United States was heavily involved in the war, Intelligence gathering would be the most difficult task and weakest link in the war effort.

The Battle for Ap Boc showed that if the South Vietnamese did not intend to listen to their American advisors, the latter were serving no useful role. American advisors would have to be given command authority or they too would become discouraged and lose the desire to continue supporting the South Vietnamese. One thing was certain after Ap Boc. The morale among the advisors fell to a critical low. Although the battle was officially reported as a courageous, determined fight against the guerrilla enemy, which ultimately ended in victory, more and more news reports revealed the real situation and American officials in South Vietnam were accused of glossing over the shortcomings revealed by the whole operation.

The battle only seemed to worsen the conflict between Diem and the news correspondents. A loud outcry was made which called for a halt to any further support to Diem. Why should the United States have already forfeited 50 American lives and more than 400,000,000 dollars with only a corrupt government, a South Vietnamese army that would not fight, and a nation in chaos where the guerrillas ruled the countryside and the people hated the government, to show for it? During this questioning period one statement more than any other would influence the direction of the war – 'Either the US should get out,' which was only media rhetoric, 'Or the US should take control and win this war,' which was precisely the mood of the Kennedy administration and the military.

Differing opinions are expressed about what next occurred, but the fact was that Diem had to be removed from the government. He had become an embarrassment and there was a strong chance that the press would turn the American people and Congress against further involvement in Vietnam. It was also possible that the Communist movement would succeed due to corruption and mishandling of

Below : a South Vietnamese patrol files across a makeshift bridge. The permanent structure was demolished by the VC.
Right : two VC prisoners look on while an ARVN patrol searches a sugar mill for hidden weapons in 1964.

the war effort by the Diem regime. President Kennedy was not willing to suffer such a foreign policy setback because of one uncontrollable Vietnamese leader. Some of the power of the Kennedy charisma had already begun to fade with the American people and the government. The Bay of Pigs fiasco and Laos stood as failures in his conduct of foreign affairs. Campaigning for the 1964 presidential elections was underway and the incumbent president could afford neither a disaster in Vietnam nor the ill will of the press. It seemed as though Kennedy had to prove himself a true leader both at home and abroad, which at times sent him on a reckless course with many of his policies and programs.

In the light of Kennedy's need to prove himself a great leader, and Diem's refusal to change policy, an excuse had to be found to 'eliminate' the South Vietnamese leader. That excuse was provided by the unrest of the Buddhist minority in May 1963. The Buddhists in South Vietnam had been in constant conflict with the Catholic majority, whose position and power was buttressed by Diem. The incident that brought about the confrontation concerned government officials permitting the minority Catholic population of Hue to fly religious flags over the city in honor of the Archbishop's birthday. Although this in itself was not of great importance other than as an irritation to the Buddhists, on 3 June 1963 the Buddhist population of Hue was banned from displaying their religious flags to honor the birthday of Buddha. The Archbishop was also Diem's brother and the local officials of Hue wished only to please the Diem regime.

The discrimination was blatant. City officials, not wishing to lose favor or show weakness in what they considered an insignificant squabble, or have Diem see their weakness and remove them from office, refused to hear the Buddhist complaint. As a result the Buddhists went onto the streets in protest. The response from the government was swift and brutal. The army, noted as little more than an extension of Diem, was called out to silence the protests. The demonstrations were dispersed with nine Buddhists slain.

Throughout the summer of 1963 clashes between government troops and Buddhists continued in all the major cities in South Vietnam. However, the most important demonstration came when Buddhist monks took to the streets and in a passive display of their subjugation drenched themselves in gasoline and set themselves on fire. The reaction of the Diem family was one of unconcern and in some cases open mockery, but the Buddhists managed to attract one audience Diem could not ignore, the media. Correspondents who witnessed and attempted to report such scenes as the Buddhist suicides were again stifled by the censors. Diem not only refused them access to troubled areas, but in some cases the National Police restrained the reporters, confiscated their material and had them beaten. With materials being confiscated by the government, many correspondents resorted to smuggling film and dispatches by way of American aircrews, who were disenchanted by what they had seen in Vietnam.

During this time reports were often inaccurate and slanted against Diem, but they caught the attention of the American people, who for the first time began to realize that perhaps all was not well in Southeast Asia. Reporters not only wanted to inform the world of the situation in Vietnam but had a score to settle with Diem that would ultimately bring his world crashing down around him.

Below left: a favorite VC booby trap was the mace, hidden in a tree with a trip wire attached to it. It was reputedly capable of knocking out a squad of troops. This example was used to train inexperienced US soldiers. Below: newly arrived US troops are shown how the VC mine a footbridge by ARVN infantrymen.

The White House could no longer sit idly by. First, Kennedy decided to relieve Nolting as ambassador, replacing him with Henry Cabot Lodge. Lodge, along with General Paul Harkins, chief US military commander, began looking elsewhere for leadership in the South Vietnamese government. Although Lodge at first tried to work with Diem, he soon realized that Diem's attitude would never alter. At the same time General Harkins was inclined to believe that a coup d'état by the generals of the ARVN could overthrow the government, but it would result in a less stable situation. That apparently left the US with only one option – Diem or nothing.

At this point the facts become uncertain. Although various coups were obviously considered in high circles, no one element or group was prepared for such a takeover. A problem was also created when Lodge's 'official' policy of noninvolvement was leaked to many of the men who might have formulated such a coup. The only stipulation that the American government made for those who might choose to revolt was that they have the support of the majority of the people and the will to fight the Communists.

On 1 November 1963 the Presidential Palace in Saigon was surrounded by rebellious generals, led by General Duong Van Minh. They demanded the immediate surrender of Diem and his brother. After a brief confrontation Diem and his brother escaped through a secret passage into the city, fleeing to the Chinese quarter. Diem remained in contact with the rebel generals and it is said that they offered him safe conduct and exile. Realizing that their situation was hopeless Diem and his brother surrendered to the generals on those conditions. Once they were in the hands of the officers, both men were executed. Though first reports stated that the brothers had committed 'accidental' suicide, no one believed the story. The rest of the Diem family, who had ruled the corrupt government, were scattered throughout the world, except for one brother who sought refuge in the American Consulate in Hue. He was later handed over to the South Vietnamese authorities and executed.

It is now widely accepted that the coup, although officially without American backing except in conscience, was instigated and strongly supported by the US Government and the CIA. Ironically, only three weeks' later, on 22 November 1963, President John F Kennedy would die from an assassin's bullet. His death shocked the world and caused deep mourning in many circles, but the Diem family in exile undoubtedly were not among the mourners.

Above left: the South Vietnamese leaders celebrate Independence Day. The head of state, Phan Khac Suu, is flanked by Maj Gen Duong Van Minh (left) and Maj Gen Nguyen Khanh. Left: troops march past in review.

General Duong Van Minh was nominated as head of the government by Diem's former vice-president, Nguyen Ngoc Tho. The nomination was made official and with 'Big Minh' controlling the government the United States obviously looked for a change in policy. Unfortunately nothing really changed. The people loyal to Diem were no longer in power, but they had simply been replaced by Big Minh's own puppets.

The Viet Cong took full advantage of the chaos in the South Vietnamese government and increased their offensive in the countryside, particularly against small government bases and fortified hamlets. By January 1964 students were rioting in the streets of Saigon. Civil unrest was growing and there were even rumors that Big Minh was about to sell out to the Communists. The chaos and need for stability could only mean another changeover. On 30 January 1964 Major General Nguyen Khanh carried out a successful bloodless coup to remove Big Minh.

The American government was deeply concerned. The chaos that reigned throughout South Vietnam would ultimately lead to its collapse and another American failure. President Johnson made it known that the United States was in full support of General Khanh's new government. Stability in Vietnam at any price was necessary and Johnson was willing to support anyone he thought could establish order from the chaos.

It was at this time that the questioning of the justice of the United State's involvement in South Vietnam must begin. It was no longer keeping a people free from Communism. Communism was merely an excuse used by Kennedy and his successor Johnson to demonstrate their power as American presidents. Johnson would manipulate the war to his own best interests, when he could, as Kennedy had done. When he could not he would apply whatever force was needed to save the honor of the American people and feed his ego. Johnson had been thrust into the presidency and realized that any chance he had to be elected to that office in the forthcoming elections would depend to no small extent on his management of the situation in Vietnam.

Johnson ordered increased aid to the government of South Vietnam, but in March 1964 Secretary of Defense MacNamara visited the country and saw that the situation continued to deteriorate rapidly. There was no stability in the government and there were rumors of further coups. Some definite policy or action on the part of the United States was needed to stop the deterioration of the government. After receiving MacNamara's report Johnson decided on the aid program he would adopt. Another 60,000,000 dollars would be added to the money already budgeted for South Vietnam. He promised to update the Vietnamese equipment, especially their aircraft and armored fighting vehicles. The United States would also assume all the costs of a 50,000-man increase to the ARVN forces.

Although this aid was simply a scaling-up of past policies, Johnson embarked on another plan – retaliatory air strikes against North Vietnam. Johnson and his advisors agreed that this would help ease the Communist pressure on South Vietnam and would display an active, positive commitment to Khanh's supporters. Even more importantly, it would prove to the North that the United States was not willing to let South Vietnam fall. But Johnson, with his close advisors, was acting on his own in planning the air attacks on North Vietnam. Neither Congress nor the American people had as yet approved such a policy. As President and Commander in Chief of the Armed Forces, Johnson saw the bombing plans as within his rights and as a quick means to regain lost ground in American foreign policy.

Timing was the delicate issue. If Johnson went ahead immediately with the bombing it would portray him as an advocate of war in Vietnam. He did not want to appear to be provoking a war with election so near. If he could delay without suffering a major embarrassment in Southeast Asia until after the election in November, then he could act and appear not as a warmonger but as the defender of freedom and democracy throughout the world.

In July 1964 circumstances in South Vietnam again grew critical. General Khanh was becoming more aggressive in his demands on the United States. He had been informed about the planned bombings and felt that there should be no more delays. He struck out through the press at the apparent lack of concern in the United States for the plight of the Vietnamese people. He kept repeating that South Vietnam was at war alone against the Communists. He contended that the only way the war could be ended was by driving north to defeat the Communist plague at its point of origin.

Below: this soldier of the 9th Infantry Division aims his M-16 rifle, which is fitted with a Starlight Scope for night firing.
Bottom left: troops of the 11th Armored Cavalry Regiment guard a VC suspect at Long Binh.
Bottom far left: the strain and fatigue of combat shows on the face of this US soldier.

Above: a group of South Vietnamese trainees practice firing the .30-caliber machine gun on the range.
Right: fortified bunkers each holding 11 men were constructed at Bien Hoa for the men of Bravo Company, 2nd Bn, 16th Infantry Regiment.

Other members of Khanh's government and military took up the cry. General Nguyen Cao Ky, commander of the South Vietnamese Air Force, said that his pilots were ready and anxious to retaliate against the North and that for every act of aggression by the guerrillas, South Vietnam should strike a blow against the North. The fact was that at that time neither the South Vietnamese nor the United States had any reliable evidence that the North Vietnamese government had combat troops fighting in the South. It was obvious that support was filtering into the South along the Ho Chi Minh Trail through Laos and Cambodia, and even along the coast of South Vietnam, but that support was confined to the weapons and equipment the Viet Cong needed to carry on the struggle.

Johnson decided that the most immediate solution, or more correctly the appearance of action, was the replacement of Ambassador Lodge with Maxwell D Taylor and the assignment of General William C Westmoreland as commander in charge of the US military presence in South Vietnam. On the surface it seemed that the South Vietnamese were calling for war on a grand scale. In fact they were calling for more positive action of the sort that had already taken place. Unknown to most, as General Ky had hinted in his statements to the press, clandestine raids had already been made against North Vietnam by land, sea and air. What General Ky had alluded to was the highly sensitive OPLAN 34A. A combined US and South Vietnamese effort, OPLAN 34A involved covert operations against North Vietnam using the methods of destruction and terrorism that the Viet Cong was applying to the South. It was a 'fight fire with fire' approach to goad the North into action. The tactics included kidnapping North Vietnamese personnel and officials to glean Intelligence information, commando raids and deploying psychological warfare teams whose purpose was to disrupt normal and military uses of roads, bridges and ports and to harass the provincial governments and the North Vietnamese people. The commando raids were carried out by South Vietnamese and Nationalist Chinese volunteers, while USAF U-2 reconnaissance flights crossed the skies of North Vietnam.

The second part of OPLAN 34A called for 25–40 bombers, with Royal Laotian markings, flown by American and Thai Air Force pilots, to take off from Laos and strike targets in North Vietnam. Part three of OPLAN 34A would send American destroyers to the Gulf of Tonkin off North Vietnam.

It was the final part of OPLAN 34A that was to give the Johnson Administration the excuse it needed to take the United States openly into the war. On 2 August, 1964 the destroyer USS *Maddox* was attacked by three North Vietnamese navy patrol boats. Although the attack had accomplished nothing and the patrol boats were easily driven away, it had been launched in retaliation for a South Vietnamese Marine attack more than 200 miles north of the demilitarized zone (DMZ). Two days' later the North Vietnamese navy once again attacked the destroyers USS *Maddox* and USS *Turner Joy*. The destroyers suffered no damage, but after a four-hour engagement two North Vietnamese vessels were sunk and two others heavily damaged.

On 5 August 1964 American aircraft from the carriers *Constellation* and *Ticonderoga* retaliated by bombing North Vietnamese naval installations, destroying more than 25 vessels. A large oil-storage site was also targeted. Two aircraft were lost during those missions and with their loss the operations could no longer be kept quiet. On 7 August the North Vietnamese Peoples Army began moving troops south toward the DMZ. That action and the reports of the attacks on American vessels by the North Vietnamese Navy led the Johnson Administration to produce its Southeast Asian Resolution, better known as the Gulf of Tonkin Resolution.

The resolution pledged full support to South Vietnam, not only in aid but also in the use of US combat troops. This document, signed into law on 11 August 1964, would give Johnson a free hand to take any steps necessary to assist the government of South Vietnam in their war effort. The Gulf of Tonkin Resolution was carefully worded so that it was not a declaration of war, which could possibly draw the Soviet Union or Peoples Republic of China into the conflict. However, the resolution provided for all the contingencies necessary to allow the United States to virtually take over the war in Vietnam. It seems obvious that the meticulously worded, well-considered phrasing of the resolution did not come overnight and that the document was already prepared and just waiting for the right incident so that it could be produced.

The Southeast Asian Resolution was thrust through Congress with the justification that the United States had been attacked and that the aggressive Communists in North Vietnam were expanding the war. The United States on the other hand was only coming to the aid of an ally. It is now known that it was the United States which provoked the North into attacks in the Gulf of Tonkin. The two destroyers were poison pawns in the game being played and were operating well within the 15-mile limit previously established as North Vietnamese waters. By antagonizing the North, Johnson had gained the ability to commit troops to South Vietnam as he saw fit.

For the following 10 weeks before the elections Johnson was cautious. Although he sent more support to South Vietnam he did not want to appear anxious to send the United States to war. In fact, Johnson assured the American people that it was not his intention to send young men to Southeast Asia, while using Senator Barry Goldwater's hard line against the North Vietnamese against the Senator.

With the defeat of Barry Goldwater in the November elections, Johnson was free to act as he had always intended. Although the American people were not eager to enter the war in Vietnam, polls indicated that they were confident that the United States could easily defeat the Communist aggressors in Southeast Asia. The stage was being set psychologically and militarily for full-scale combat involvement in Vietnam.

Below: troops of the US Army's 1st Air Cavalry Division await resupply helicopters during Operation Cedar Falls in January 1967.
Far left: a selection of the VC weapons captured during Operation Cedar Falls in the Iron Triangle area of South Vietnam.
Left: this VC base camp was discovered by troops of the US 11th Cavalry Div.

Below: members of the US 25th Infantry Division move into the village of Vinh Cu in search of suspected Viet Cong, April 1966.

American Entanglement

From the Gulf of Tonkin Incident in 1964 until the Tet Offensive of 1968 the Vietnam Conflict would require more commitment than was ever foreseen. After studying the situation during his 1964 visit MacNamara concluded that the war would be over in five years. The first few years would probably be spent stabilizing the South Vietnamese government and directing it toward the social reforms which would ultimately lead to the stabilization of the country. The problems of the Vietnamese people would have to be attended to before the guerrillas could be defeated. The quieting of unrest was of primary importance. However, MacNamara though paying lip service to the idea, used social reforms as a bargaining point between the United States and South Vietnamese governments. American aid and funds would be the bait to obtain goals in social reforms.

However, such reforms were essential and the American government failed in all its years in Vietnam to see that programs for the betterment of the people were implemented. A large portion of the Vietnamese viewed the South Vietnamese government as a greater enemy than the guerrilla. There was a sympathetic saying among advisors who worked with the South Vietnamese that describes the situation very clearly. 'The VC may come and take their food and sleep in their house, but the government soldier will come and take their food, burn their house and beat them.' The second phase of the 'MacNamara Five Year Plan' would see the enormous US war machine eliminating all guerrilla activity in the country, building up a strong ARVN military similar to that of the South Koreans, and perhaps the balance would tip so much in favor of the South that the people of the North might rebel against the Communist masters.

Although MacNamara had the situation wrapped up in a neat package, in actual fact conditions in South Vietnam were as chaotic as ever. Ambassador Taylor had informed Washington that the situation in the government and military of South Vietnam was decaying rapidly. He felt that a genuine state of emergency existed and the only way to offset that was for the United States to involve itself to a greater extent in the war effort. This meant that some degree of escalation would have to occur. The political situation in South Vietnam was linked so delicately to the war effort that its stability could only be guaranteed by a show of strength. President Johnson continued to have a problem with exactly how he could show strength and support without portraying himself as the antagonist. The idea of air strikes as a retaliation against any action taken by the guerrilla in the South was still viewed as the prime option, but General Khanh's government continued to advocate the 'march north and destroy' concept, which would mean US combat involvement.

Johnson finally acceded to Taylor's proposals concerning the air strikes as a means of showing the Communists that no aggression would go unpunished, but he maintained a tight control on the numbers and locations of the bombing raids which would take place. Although the Gulf of Tonkin Incident had been one situation which could be used to advocate greater military support for the South, it still was not enough in itself to bring about a full-scale US military involvement. A rallying point was needed, which would enable Johnson to deploy American troops with the backing of the United States people. Johnson realized that he must tread softly and maintain his image as a protector rather than appear as an aggressor.

Above: USAF security police repel an attack on Tan Son Nhut Air Base.
Left: 105mm howitzers of 2nd Bn 19th Artillery are positioned on a ridge overlooking the Vinh Thanh Valley.

In late December 1964 the first air actions of notable scale, dubbed Operation Barrel-Roll took place. These strikes were directed solely against the Ho Chi Minh Trail in Laos. Such a limited operation was in keeping with Johnson's immediate course, yet publicly it seemed to indicate that he was demonstrating great support and

restraint with the use of military force.

Vietnamese politics again became the most important issue, when a group of young officers calling themselves Young Turks became disillusioned with the Khanh regime. Although they had originally supported General Khanh, their disenchantment with him was growing with each day. The young officers wanted action. One of their leaders, General Nguyen Cao Ky approached the American Consulate and General Westmoreland. He informed the Americans that the rebellious officers felt that a change was needed and that Khanh was no longer effective as a leader owing to his many compromises with the Buddhist faction and other elements of the government. Both Ambassador Taylor and General Westmoreland realized the severity of the situation and worked diligently to increase US aid, which would appease the officers, and to resolve a compromise between the factions. They asked all parties concerned to work in harmony for the betterment of the country.

Peace existed only on the surface. The 'Young Turks' were calling for Khanh to do away with many of his senior staff and generals. After believing that they had struck a bargain on the issue, they discovered that Khanh had no intention of removing the men. The situation was only brought under control when Taylor himself reprimanded the officers and General Ky, calling them school boys and threatening to discontinue aid if they persisted. The Young Turks were furious with Taylor's treatment, but they could do very little. Taylor then approached General Khanh and suggested that the general may have outlived his usefulness and even went so far as to offer him retirement in exile. General Khanh was infuriated by the suggestion and not only lashed out at the ambassador with a show of strength by his officer corps, but related his meeting with Taylor to a correspondent of the *New York Herald Tribune Review*.

Khanh's retaliation backfired when the US State Department stood behind the ambassador and let it be known to all parties concerned that the United States was not willing to tolerate much more of the petty squabbling and instability within the government. It was clear that the United States government no longer considered Khanh capable of managing the situation, or able to utilize properly the aid that the United States was lavishing on the South Vietnamese.

While tempers flared between the

two governments, the Viet Cong bombed an hotel in Saigon on Christmas Eve. The attack left three Americans dead and 51 Americans and South Vietnamese injured. This VC act of terrorism only seemed to confirm the strong words of Secretary of State Dean Rusk on the incompetency of Khanh's government.

After that incident Ambassador Taylor again approached President Johnson, suggesting that he begin retaliatory air strikes against North Vietnam, citing the Saigon bombing as just provocation. Johnson delayed the decision, as he believed that some might claim that the bombing had been engineered by Khanh, not the Viet Cong. Johnson needed evidence that it was a VC outrage, not so much for himself, but for the American press and people. Although Johnson had been reelected he had not yet been inaugurated. Bombing North Vietnam at that time would have been an extreme reaction. What he could and would do was use this incident to end the squabbling among the South Vietnamese generals and, when the right time came, begin the air offensive against the North.

Johnson's threats against the feuding members of the South Vietnamese government worked perfectly. Khanh and his officers compromised and returned the country to a civil gov-

Below: members of the Vietnamese National Police search Bong Son village for VC, escorted by men of the US 1st Cavalry Division (Air Mobile). Right: Major Ben Crosby of the 25th Infantry Division locates a bamboo breathing tube leading from an underground VC hideout near Duc Pho. Below right: a camouflaged VC tunnel was discovered and later destroyed by the US 196th Light Infantry Brigade near Dao Tinh in 1966.

Below: Vietnamese civilians evacuate their homes as ARVN Rangers move in on VC terrorists during the Communist Tet Offensive in 1968.

Far left: a 'tunnel rat' is helped from the entrance to a VC underground-tunnel complex discovered during a search-and-destroy mission.
Left: a private of 173rd Airborne Brigade uses a sewing machine salvaged from a VC tunnel.
Below: an artist's impression of a VC HQ tunnel complex, based on that discovered 25 miles northwest of Saigon in January 1966. The building in the foreground covers a tunnel entrance and two machine guns have been mounted at the bottom of the wall. The tunnel affords protection from airstrikes and artillery fire, while the outer zigzag trenches defend the base from attack by infantry. The cone-shaped hole in the right foreground is an AA-gun emplacement.
Below: 'tunnel rats' on a search mission uncover training aids used by the VC to teach recruits how to install booby traps.
Bottom: US troops check an apparently innocent village well, which may conceal the entrance to a VC tunnel.

ernment under Premier Tran Van Huong. Unfortunately, while the compromise solved one problem it created another. The Buddhists announced that, while they were willing to cooperate with Khanh, they would not cooperate with the new civilian government. With the arrival of the new year civil unrest had increased. The Buddhists returned to the type of demonstrations they had used during the Diem regime and in January alone 65 Buddhists burned themselves alive in the streets, one of them a girl of only 17 years of age. By 27 January 1965 the Buddhists had caused the collapse of the civil government and the generals called for Khanh to return to power.

Chaos is the only description for the state of affairs in the South Vietnamese government. As government succeeded government in an effort to bring about order, the Viet Cong saw an opportune moment to strike. In a four-day battle near Saigon VC guerrillas, armed with new weapons from the North, occupied the village of Binh Gia, killing six Americans and 177 ARVN troops. The battle ended only when the Communist troops voluntarily withdrew, not because of the actions of the government troops sent to repel them.

The battle caused the United States command in Vietnam to review its situation. General Westmoreland was certain that the Viet Cong had introduced new large-scale tactics and would no longer be satisfied with the minor guerrilla activities that had been common in the past. As a result of the state of chaos throughout the country, a growing anti-American feeling, more-conventional large-scale attacks by the VC and attacks against American personnel, the US Government would have to act, and act swiftly, to establish order. Taylor again advocated the bombing of the North. Although the Johnson staff agreed that air strikes might be the answer Johnson again refused to authorize the reprisal attacks until something more sensational could be used to justify them. He was playing his hand beautifully, allowing the anger of the American people to grow.

Finally, shortly after the Tet Holiday Truce, the Viet Cong attacked the US Advisory Compound at Pleiku,

Opposite: US Army advisors to a Civilian Irregular Defense Unit accompany their troops on a patrol from Camp Thoung Duc in 1967. Above left: a patrol leader signals his men to stop and take cover. Left: this grenade booby trap was part of the defenses of the Tran Sup Checkpoint in Tay Ninh.

killing two Americans and wounding 126. The VC also struck in Binh Dinh Province causing a death toll of more than 450, with an unknown number of ARVN wounded. What gave the raid critical importance was that it followed immediately after the truce and seemed to be deliberate displays of strength while the Soviet Premier Alexei Kosygin was visiting Hanoi. President Johnson had his 'sensational incident.' He used those attacks, tying them to what would appear as marked Soviet influence, to state that the United States had no choice but to retaliate against the communist aggressors of North Vietnam in support of its South Vietnamese allies.

The United States then embarked on an air war which would have two primary purposes. The first was retaliation. The second was to strike at 94 major industrial and military targets in the North to destroy the ability of the North Vietnamese to support the war effort. It was truly believed that once the United States had received just provocation for employing strategic bombing of North Vietnam the end of the war would be in sight; that the air war alone would defeat the Communists and bring about the chance the South needed to achieve order and stability. A great deal was dependent on the success of the bombing of North Vietnam.

Westmoreland was concerned about the ability of the ARVN to protect the US air bases, particularly at Da Nang as that airfield would become a primary target of the VC forces. As a direct result of the concern for the security of the bases, on 26 February 1965 President Johnson approved a bill for the commitment of US ground forces to Vietnam. Their primary function was the defense of Da Nang.

On 8 March 1965 the 9th Marine Expeditionary Brigade, commanded by Brigadier General Frederick J Karch, landed at Da Nang. In true Marine spirit the brigade assaulted China Beach, which ran along the small peninsula near the city of Da Nang. The ironic part of this whole episode was that as the first combat troops assaulted the first beach in Vietnam in full battle array, they were met by city officials from Da Nang, curious Vietnamese, Special Forces advisors with their South Vietnamese troops and groups of well-wishing American airmen who had erected signs of welcome. A full combat assault was made to the cheers of a beer-drinking crowd. The signs 'Welcome

Left: two riflemen of the 173rd Airborne Division charge VC positions in a wooded area in Zone 'D' of South Vietnam.

Above: a platoon commander of the US 3rd Marine Division encourages his men in the pursuit of North Vietnamese Regular Army troops. Left: US infantrymen go to the aid of a wounded comrade in a rice paddy. Above right: a US infantryman waits for his squad to catch him up.

Gallant Marines' would remain timely reminders as an ever-increasing flow of American troops joined the fighting in Vietnam.

The floodgates were open. Johnson had managed to surmount the final obstacles that stood in the way of the American takeover of the war effort. He felt relatively confident that the United States would be viewed by the rest of the world, or at least by its allies, not as the power escalating the war, but as the one who was attempting to end it. Communist expansionism was being felt around the world and in one small corner of it at least, the United States intended to stop that expansion.

No sooner had the Marines landed at Da Nang than more reinforcements were authorized. On 8 June Australian troops arrived, Australia being one of the SEATO allies who would join the American effort in Vietnam. American troops were given the freedom to make offensive patrols and were no longer restricted to the role of guarding American installations. New Zealand forces would soon arrive, as the

United States put pressure on the SEATO allies to fulfill their obligations to that organization.

By the end of June American, South Vietnamese and Australian troops began to work in close cooperation on what would be known as 'search and destroy' missions. These missions were designed primarily to sweep given areas to dislodge and engage any guerrilla forces and to 'pacify' the area by showing support for the local population. Search and destroy would for the first time attempt to prove that the guerrillas were no longer safe in the countryside. Although that was the purpose, it would later become evident that the goals were not always accomplished.

July 1965 witnessed another influx of American troops with the 1st Infantry Division and the 101st Airborne Division arriving 'in country.' By September, the 1st Cavalry Division (Air Mobile) arrived in An Khe. Within a time span of less than three months the United States had changed from a policy of advisory support and aid to one of total combat commitment. That commitment brought new strategies, or what were thought to be new strategies, to end the fighting.

First the air war would be continued and escalated. It was believed that it would take from three to five divisions to put a halt to the transportation of supplies from the North along the Ho Chi Minh Trail. However, to commit those troops could be disastrous in the long run and the possibility of an American Dien Bien Phu struck a sour note. In any event the United States Air Force was considered without equal in the world. Applying air power to the interdiction of the supply line should easily contain and decrease the amount of supplies which could travel along that route.

With that aspect of the strategy resolved, the ground troops would be free to engage the guerrillas. The strategy for the American ground war was as basic as for the air war. Divisions would establish themselves in heavily fortified bases along the coast at Phu Bai, Da Nang, Chui Lai, Qui Nhon and Cam Ranh. The concept was that strong fortified bases along the coastline would be easy to resupply and impossible to cut off.

Smaller base camps of battalion and company strength were placed at designated intervals surrounding the larger bases to maintain their integrity by providing greater depth of defense. The secondary bases were placed in such a manner that through the use of heavy support weapons, primarily artillery, they could support one another and the troops in the field. From those bases American troops would operate either large-scale missions against known enemy strongholds (reconnaissance in force), or the smaller search and destroy missions.

As American involvement in Vietnam began to escalate various problems were posed and solutions sought. The United States government had not only found an area of the world where it could confront and destroy Communism but it had engaged in a war abroad while there was peace at home. Owing to this, the United States military machine could experiment with and perfect new weapons and tactics at its leisure, unhampered by the pressures from a wartime domestic government.

The United States also had what it considered to be the ultimate innovation for fighting guerrillas – the fortified base. Although the French had used the fortified base concept, they had been restricted in supplying and supporting those bases to either the use of the roadways, which only truly existed along the coast and went inland only to link with major cities or villages, or the use and deployment of paratroopers. Although the paratroops could be dropped into an area to surprise the enemy they had several handicaps. These ranged from supply to support ability, but most crucial of all was the inability to extract the troops once the operation was either completed or aborted. In most cases those troops were forced to march or fight their way out.

The United States military felt that the key to fighting the guerrilla hinged on the ability to put troops in and out at will, striking at the enemy on his own ground, but on your terms. The key to such a capability was the helicopter. This addition to the military arsenal requires examination if this aspect of the military strategy is to be understood.

For years after World War II and the establishment of the USAF as a separate branch of the military, the army found itself in a constant dispute over whether or not the army could retain aircraft which it felt were essential for observation and the immediate support of soldiers in the field. Many members of the army believed that the Air Force should concern itself strictly with strategic bombing and destroying the enemy's air capability, but that the army should retain those aircraft whose role it was to give close-combat support to ground troops. Experience had taught the military that the fewer commanders there were, the less chance of error and the better the support. It is implied that everything in the service must be for the good of the soldier but, as the combat troop can attest, it somehow never works out quite that way. The army did not want to lose the new 'wonder weapon,' the aircraft. Yet because of the division of the services it had no choice.

In 1952 experiments began with the use of the helicopter in various aspects of warfare. Its initial usefulness was confined to three main areas: the helicopter served as a means of swift reconnaissance; it could be used to direct artillery firing into forward areas; and it could transport small quantities of supplies to the front with great speed. The primitive state of helicopters at that time prohibited the transportation of heavy loads, which cargo aircraft could drop in, but the helicopter had the ability to deliver supplies directly to the troops. This made the helicopter far more valuable than the cargo aircraft, which often missed its dropping zones and rendered the supplies useless to troops who needed them most desperately.

Perhaps the most important aspect of the helicopter was its ability to land and take off in a relatively small ground space. The helicopter could be used to evacuate wounded soldiers, taking them from the front to medical facilities in a matter of minutes, which would without a doubt save many lives. It was this one role which probably won more favor for the helicopter than any other. In Korea, where the helicopter was first used in appreciable numbers, it was this factor that won it the most praise.

By the mid-1950s the military was beginning to change its views and attitudes towards warfare. With their experience in Korea, the army re-

alized that it needed to overcome the problems of mobilization and maneuverability of their troops in impassable terrain. The application and use of the paratrooper was being re-evaluated. Although paratroopers had a potential for great mobility, when dropped into target areas they were often scattered for miles around the actual target zone. Another factor was that they could basically only carry weapons light enough to be dropped in with them. In many cases the lack of adequate heavy weapons meant the difference between success and failure. Although paratroopers had a glorious record in World War II and their activities had become legendary, they were rapidly becoming obsolete. What was really needed was a system which retained the paratroopers' mobility, but allowed them to be supplied with heavy weapons and which could leave an area as quickly as it had come.

The helicopter provided the answer and the concept of the 'Sky Cav' was born. It was obvious that if the helicopter could extract wounded troops and carry them from active battlefields, then the helicopter could take troops to and from battle sites with a mobility and accuracy that had never been possible before. The helicopter would become the flying horse of the American army and in 1959 the army began looking for a helicopter to fit the specification of a light observation, surveillance and tactical transport aircraft.

At the same time the Bell Company was in the advanced stages of developing a utility helicopter which appeared to fit the army's requirements. This helicopter was the forerunner of the UH-1 Iroquois, which would later be nicknamed the 'Huey' and would be the primary support helicopter of the Vietnam conflict. The Rogers Board, an investigative committee on helicopter feasibility, urged the army to adopt the helicopter, if only on the grounds that its range would make it effective for observation for divisional artillery.

It was not until three years later that President Kennedy's Secretary of Defense MacNamara took a special interest in the development of the helicopter and its value was finally recognized. Within three months of MacNamara's statement the Howze

Above left: ARVN troops wade through rice paddies while on a search-and-destroy mission during Operation 'Long Phi 990' in October 1966.
Far left: armored personnel carriers of the ARVN 2nd Armored Cavalry drive through rice paddies.
Left: troops of the 11th Armored Cavalry Regiment take cover as VC automatic weapons open up.

Board was established and submitted a report recommending that no less than 450 helicopters should be given to each of the five main divisions and that both UH-1 and Boeing CH-47 Chinooks cargo helicopters should be used. The two models would each have a specific function. The Huey was to be used as a troop carrier and modified as, a gunship for initial and support attacks. The Chinooks would be used as a heavy cargo helicopter capable of lifting divisional artillery weapons and even some light-missile artillery to support what would be known as the Air Assault Division.

In January 1963 at Fort Benning, Georgia, the concept was used in the formation of the 11th Air Assault Division, which would in later years be reconstituted into the 1st Cavalry Division (Air Mobile) on its way to combat in Vietnam.

The basic tactics devised for the helicopter in Vietnam would follow a prescribed sequence of actions. A landing zone (LZ) would be selected in the immediate area of the assault. The Huey helicopters would then carry troops, flying at a speed of approximately 115 miles per hour just above the tree tops, toward the selected LZ. Upon reaching the zone, those helicopters armed as gunships would lay fire around the LZ with machine guns and rockets to eliminate any enemy resistance, clearing the way for the troop assault helicopters. The gunships would then take up stations above the LZ, hovering in support, while the assault 'birds' unloaded their troops. If any resistance was encountered before the assault landing was completed, the gunships would target the areas marked out by colored smoke cannisters laid by the ground troops to indicate the approximate enemy position.

Once the assault troops were in position the helicopters would return to their base, refuel and wait until the ground troops had completed their missions. They would then fly out and retrieve the assault troops. When all went well, missions of this nature could be handled with quick, precise efficiency. If the operation was of a more permanent nature, such as the establishment of a fire-support base, the heavier cargo Chinooks could bring in supplies, artillery and even the building materials required to construct a fortification.

The helicopter gave commanders the capability to put troops anywhere they wished with a hitherto un-

Left: two members of 4th Battalion, 503rd Infantry Regiment wait for the helicopter which will evacuate the body of a comrade.

Left: members of a government Revolutionary Development team help refugees to build temporary shacks in June 1966.
Below left: a soldier of the 101st Airborne Division guards Vietnamese farmers as they gather the rice crop in Phu Yen Province.
Right: psychological warfare was an important part of the fight against the VC. Here a loudspeaker team prepare to broadcast.
Far right: a Vietnamese Cultural Civic Action Team reconstruct a small footbridge destroyed by flooding at Thai Binh in 1966.
Below: a US civil-affairs officer shows a Vietnamese child his stethoscope, Pleiku, 1966.

Left: the Revolutionary Development Center at Vung Tau gave South Vietnamese volunteers practical training for development work.
Below left: paratroopers of the 173rd Airborne Brigade bring their mortar into action.
Above: a VC artist's view of an American soldier found in a deserted village by the 173rd Airborne Bde.
Below: 'Dusters' were tank bodies fitted with 40mm cannon.

precedented speed, pinpoint accuracy and mobility. It also enabled the commander to extract troops just as rapidly if the situation so warranted. Owing to this factor the helicopter was viewed by troops as a far-reaching umbilical cord that could sustain them in combat. No GI who saw combat in Vietnam will ever forget the feeling of relief when he heard the sound of a 'chopper' coming in. Whether it was on a mission to extract troops from an operation, collect wounded, bring supplies or as support when a gunship came on station to help beat back the enemy, the helicopter was a welcome sight.

As previously mentioned, there were only two basic infantry offensive tactics employed in Vietnam: reconnaissance in force; and search and destroy. Reconnaissance in force usually involved a battalion or more of men, Americans and South Vietnamese, whose basic purpose was to move through an area where Intelligence reports indicated the enemy was active. Their function was to engage and destroy the enemy forces in pitched battles and ultimately to clear the entire sector of enemy troops. After the successful completion of that mission the area cleared was to be considered pacified.

Unlike the reconnaissances in force, which were coordinated operations with long-range objectives, the search-and-destroy missions were the common day-to-day actions. Generally such missions were executed by units from platoon to company size and were concerned only with maintaining the security of a given area. Ninety percent of search-and-destroy missions ended in frustration. Seldom would a unit actually engage the enemy. Moreover it was usually a case of the enemy harassing the unit, rather than the unit harassing the enemy. So the VC would simply melt away and wait until the troops had passed through their area and then return for 'business as usual.' The main problem was that the largest proportion of American and ARVN casualties came from just this type of mission. The men fell prey to ambush, snipers, boobytraps, and mines, while at the same time never actually coming to grips with the enemy. The success of the search and destroy missions was very limited, and were, needless to say, extremely unpopular with the American troops, who had to perform them on almost a

24

Above left and above: armored personnel carriers operated on search-and-destroy missions. Left: this 105mm howitzer was mounted on a converted landing craft to provide artillery support from the Saigon River.

daily basis.

The last component of the developing tactics was the fire-support base, or simply fire base. These bases were not only intended to be the first line of defense for the large fortified bases of the divisions, but were also operational centers which could function independently in their areas to attack and harass the enemy. The positioning of the bases was dependent on their objective. Some were positioned near major lines of infiltration to curb the use of such routes and cut the enemy lines of supply and communication. Others were positioned near known VC concentrations, or key areas of enemy operations, in a effort to engage and destroy the enemy. It was from the fire-support bases that most search-and-destroy missions were run, as the mission could derive artillery support and quick reinforcements from the base if a major confrontation should develop.

A fire-support base was generally laid out in a circular pattern and comprised three basic elements. The first was a battery of guns, ranging from heavy mortars and 105mm Howitzers to self-propelled 8-inch guns. The artillery was usually revetted and surrounded with sandbags for maximum protection in the event of the base coming under fire. The second element was the tactical operations center (TOC), which was the command and Intelligence gathering headquarters for the base and which had the responsibility of coordinating the operations of the base functions and orchestrating support roles in which the base was involved. The third element was the troops who manned and protected the fire base; divided into the troops who manned the guns, the supply and operational personnel who maintained the base and the infantryman who were attached to the base for defense security and daily operations. The size of the fire base usually determined the number of infantry troops who would be assigned to the base. If the base were relatively small and in a good defensible position, a troop strength of several platoons would be attached to it. If the base were larger and had the function of blocking and disrupting an area of major enemy operations then a company or battalion of troops would be assigned to it.

In physical appearance a fire-support base was generally nothing more than a dirt hillock in the center of lush vegetation. Ninety percent of the base construction was dug in and below ground level. During the dry season fire bases were nothing more than dust piles and during monsoon rains it was not uncommon to sink knee deep in mud and have most of the bunkers completely flooded. Concertina wire was laid around the perimeter with two to four man bunkers placed at intervals as guard stations.

Fire bases had few comforts and after living on one for a short time it was easy to feel more like a mole than a soldier. The fire-support base concept was made possible by the ability to resupply them by cargo helicopters and to protect them with combat support which could be brought to bear by the artillery of other bases and by attack aircraft and helicopters which were generally no more than a few minutes away. Their roles and abilities made them a persistent thorn in the side of the VC and many of these bases became prime targets of the enemy.

Although the support system of the fire-support bases was elaborate and well orchestrated, the main problem that faced them was the weather. If the enemy could wait until the rains or bad weather set in, the fire-support base would lose its crucial support from the air and a strong attack in regimental strength could overrun the smaller bases.

Although this description of a fire-support base, with its artillery, bunker

systems, and helipads gives the official picture, many were a far cry from this in actual fact. Any hill that was taken by American forces and which was considered to be in an advantageous position could become a fire-support base. Heavy mortars for support artillery and wire strung around a hill to keep the enemy out defined it as a fire-support base. The bunker system would consist of one or two hollowed, sandbagged areas, while the majority of the troops were left to dig themselves in wherever they could. This type of base was usually kept for a few days or weeks during a particular operation and was in fact nothing more than a fortified LZ.

Life on a well-established fire base was not quite as spartan as that on the smaller bases. Once a site had been established and was considered of great importance to brigade or divisional operations, a massive building program would take place. Although perhaps not uncomfortably spartan, life on any fire-support base was extremely boring and tedious. If a soldier was not carrying out some kind of duty, he would invariably be found either playing baseball or football, or sitting in his bunker blaring his radio or cassette tape player.

Boredom and frustration were the worst enemies during quiet periods. After being 'in country' for any length of time and discovering that it was not the Americans who would initiate combat but the enemy, the situation caused many of the troops to look on the war as nothing but a farce. Alcohol and drugs were used to fight the boredom and the frustration. The troops inability to relax even when there was nothing to do, and the inability at times to take the war seriously were real and dangerous problems. The American Red Cross Volunteers did their part to alleviate the monotony, but in my own experience, being supplied with coloring books and crayons and asked to join in such games as steal the bacon was hardly what I had in mind.

When the situation did become active these bases could turn into a living hell. The Viet Cong knew the state of boredom, frustration and anxiety that existed and would let these build until the troops on the bases would become almost complacent. At such times the VC knew that there was a likelihood of finding a perimeter guard bunker 'open,' because the troops were either sleeping on duty or paying little attention to their duties. When this happened the base could be attacked in two ways. The most common was the sapper attack. Specially trained VC troops would spend the night infiltrating the defenses. Once inside the wire they would attack guns, bunkers and supply areas with satchel demolition charges. In the confusion that ensued they would slip out at another point on the base. The second type of attack was not as common, but was far more devastating. The full-scale assault had the objective of over-running or destroying the base. The assaults were only conducted at night and were over before dawn. Generally the weather was such that aircraft could not be called in for support. The enemy troops would approach the perimeter, then open the attack with mortars to destroy what they could of the base defenses and, more importantly, keep the defending troops pinned down. In spite of all their training and technology, the American troops found that fighting the enemy at close quarters, especially at night, was a horrifying experience. If there was no hint that the attack was coming, half the camp would probably be sleeping. When awakened by the assault, the troops would be dazed and confused, and in those crucial initial minutes that confusion could give the enemy the time to breakthrough.

The defenders had the problem of getting enough men to the threatened sectors quickly enough to repel the attack, but if even a few of the enemy should break through the situation would become desperate. At night, with the poor visibility, confusion and panic were the worst enemy. American troops would often hold out in small groups hoping that somehow they could repel the attack and survive the night. If the situation became truly hopeless, and it appeared that the enemy intended to occupy the base and not merely overrun it to cause damage and casualties, many soldiers would take their chances by moving out into the jungle hoping to rendezvous with friendly forces or be picked up by rescue helicopters. When the situation became this desperate it was usually every man for himself. In the last resort the command post would call for artillery fire from a support base aimed directly on top of their own position, hoping to kill or drive off the enemy, while the defending troops weathered the barrage as best they could.

Any combat veteran who has experienced such an assault will never forget how terrifying or how long one night can be. The American soldier was truly unprepared for Vietnam. Long days of inactivity would erupt into a brief fire fight that would end as quickly as it had begun, unseen snipers and booby traps killed, and the situation became one not of war but of mere survival. These feelings had an impact even in the early years of the war and the command embarked on a policy designed to rely more on the advances of technology than on the efforts of the average ground soldier to win the war. Yet in the early days of the war American operations were achieving a great deal of success. The new tactics and application of weapons and technology, as well as the willingness to dispute the countryside of Vietnam with the Communists, began to build a confidence into the South Vietnamese army, government and people. Throughout 1966 and 1967 the American and ARVN forces were showing a superiority over the guerrilla forces.

The problem was that the more casualties that were incurred, the more the American people began to question the situation in Vietnam. Victories were flashed across the evening news and, although they gave a feeling of pride, they did not give a feeling of accomplishment. New methods had to be found to supplement the information that was being given. As a result, Secretary of Defense MacNamara manipulated the portrayal of the war into what can only be described as a big business venture.

One of the first things MacNamara dealt with was the replacement of combat troops. No longer would men serve together as one unit and experience war together until their unit's rotation 'stateside.' Basic units were established and replenished by a constant flow of men. The replacement/rotation process was much like an enormous assembly line. When a vacancy was opened the draft pool would fill the slot. As a result, close bonds of friendship were kept to a minimum. By confining friendships to only a few individuals fewer troops suffered from combat fatigue, and battlefield psychological disorders that had been seen in World War II. At worst one or two men in a unit would feel the loss of a close friend, as opposed to the entire unit. Although this remedied one of the immediate problems it created others which would have a lasting effect and troops began to see their combat time as a prison sentence rather than as active-duty time.

Also by the time an individual had become competent at his assigned task he was usually ready to leave, which made him become even more cautious than he had previously been. The fact that the Vietnam combat forces were not there 'for the duration' played a

Above left : an infantry squad takes cover after dismounting from its armored personnel carrier.
Left : Marines of E Company, 2nd Battalion, 3rd Marines hitch a ride on a tank.

Below: an M-48 tank of the 3rd Bn, 4th Cavalry and infantrymen of the 2nd Bn, 14th Infantry, carry out a search-and-destroy mission during Operation 'Fort Smith' in June 1966.

key role in their attitudes toward the war and the people of South Vietnam.

Another of MacNamara's new strategies for the war was the use of the abundance of technology which the United States had 'on tap.' The MacNamara Line (codenamed Duffel Bag) was established below the DMZ. It comprised fire-support bases, electronic sensors, ground surveillance radar and infantry patrols, which were all going to stop the North Vietnamese Army (NVA) from infiltrating across the DMZ. The fact was that the DMZ was not a major infiltration route, nor was the MacNamara Line difficult to circumvent.

A multitude of radar sites was established at major installations and fire-support bases to help automate the destruction of the enemy. In the Intelligence field a massive array of sophisticated devices was employed to locate the enemy. Ground-surveillance radars probed for movement at distances beyond the capabilities of standard observation. Ground sensors were planted along known infiltration points to monitor the degree of enemy activity and acquire targets for aircraft and artillery. These sensors, which operated on sound and seismic disturbances, were so delicate that artillery units occasionally fired on what they thought was an enemy infiltration but which in reality was an ant colony.

Other items included special daytime photography and nighttime infrared scanners. Two of the new items, ground sensors and infrared photography received a great deal of press

Above : one of the 69th Armored Regiment's tanks came to grief on a landmine during Operation 'Kalamazoo' near Cu Chi in 1966. Above right : a 175mm self-propelled gun of the 14th Artillery Regiment moves down a muddy road to a new location during Operation 'Seward' near Tuy Hoa in 1966.

coverage in 1970. One news story involved the interrogation of NVA soldiers who had been told by their officers that a red blanket draped over their bodies during infiltration would hide them from the infrared scanners. They also revealed that they believed ground sensors could only detect them if they talked. Therefore, by keeping quiet and walking quickly past the sensors they would be safe. The press was amused by the stories and the *Stars and Stripes*, the military newspaper in Southeast Asia, ran full picture articles showing how stupid the enemy was and explaining how the systems actually worked. Within two weeks of the printing of those articles, which should have carried a classified rating, the NVA/VC had learned their lessons and would no longer make the same mistakes. I was in Vietnam when those articles were printed and could not help but wonder what the US Army would do next to make my life easier.

The war was rapidly becoming a joint military and scientific endeavor. Whenever a military problem arose United States technology would roll another weapon off the assembly line, but some of those technological wonders began to backfire. One example is the increasing number of health problems among veterans, which has been attributed to defoliants such as Agent Orange.

If computerization and the 'corporate' approach were not enough to give recognizable proof that the American troops were establishing control over the Vietnamese countryside, it could be shown by the massive numbers of enemy casualties. MacNamara's body-count program would have far-reaching consequences, but it initially served its purpose by adding to the 'profit tables' of his 'corporate war budget.' The enormous numbers of alleged enemy losses served to give the American troops and people that feeling of accomplishment that the strict reporting of events in Vietnam did not. The enemy was being eliminated, and by comparison with the enemy losses, the casualties suffered by American troops did not seem quite so severe.

Another of MacNamara's areas of special interest was the Air Force and its application. Just as he had seen the future of the helicopter in the Army while others were still questioning it, he realized the potential of the Air Force in Vietnam. Like many other aspects of the war, the Air Force's participation would become self-propagating, looking not toward the end of the war but toward the need for new equipment and aircraft.

The Air Force was a relatively new service and to achieve its goals it was obliged to create its own war. Although the policy of mounting airstrikes as retaliation for aggressions in the South had already been established, this would mean that the Air Force would have a very limited role to play. Flying support for ground troops could be accomplished effectively with ground-attack helicopters and older propeller aircraft. The jet age Air Force had only a minor contribution to make.

Using what was almost a World War II concept of massive bombardment, the main objectives of the Air Force would be the disruption and destruction of enemy lines of supply, and later of troop infiltrations. The

main effort would be focussed on the Ho Chi Minh Trail to render it unusable through constant assault. Although the trail was bombed day and night, troops and supplies from the North were inconvenienced, never thwarted. When the trail, which was only 8–12 feet wide, became so pockmarked by bombs that it resembled a lunar landscape, the NVA/VC would simply use bulldozers or shovels to clear a path. From one bombing raid to the next it would seem that the trail would move from one side to the other of the main roadway, with the flow of transportation and supplies relatively unaffected.

Four main areas of the infiltration route were targeted. Ban Ravine, the Ban Karai Pass, Mu Gia Pass, and Ne Pa Pass were struck by air missions almost daily, yet the bombing never managed to cause a noticeable reduction in the flow of enemy support or materiel. In 1966 the Air Force even employed B-52 bombers against the Mu Gia Pass from bases in Guam. Yet bombing the Trail accomplished nothing. If an enemy convoy was caught in the bombing raid that was one thing, but the constant cratering of the Trail, which could be levelled again with machines or by hand, was profitless.

The other primary bombing objective for the Air Force was North Vietnam. The strategy behind those raids was simple: to destroy the will of the North Vietnamese people to continue their war. Military and civilian targets were struck and it seemed as though the entire military command believed that that alone would bring the North to submission. Any historian could have pointed out that the London Blitz or Allied air attacks on Germany during World War II did not bring the people to their knees, but rather made them defiant. European correspondents in Hanoi printed articles about the valiant struggles of the people in the face of the American bombardment, and if anything the air war against the North created a sympathy for the North Vietnamese and disgust for the American tactics in Southeast Asia. The Air Force did not only bomb in North Vietnam. Experiments were made with seeding the clouds over the North to create unusually high rainfall, causing floods and crop damage. Aircraft were also used to mine North Vietnamese harbors and to conduct reconnaissance and surveillance missions.

Vietnam also served as a proving ground for the comparison of American weapons and equipment with those of the Soviet Union. United States fighter aircraft perfected their tactics for fighting Soviet aircraft and learned that the missile armament that had so dominated American thinking in the development of fighter aircraft still required the backup of gun armament. The Air Force tested its electronic warfare equipment against the Soviet-built radar and missile systems and developed tactics to evade them and weapons to destroy them.

Other projects that were investigated over the course of the war included drone aircraft missions over areas considered too dangerous for manned aircraft. The airborne command post was also evaluated. This aircraft would control all of the missions involved in one day's operations from the air in the vicinity of the actual target areas. There was one area, however, where the Air Force never seemed to perfect its operations to the same degree or with the same success that it achieved with its own specific projects during the war. That was in the role of close tactical support for the ground troops. Having been in the field myself and called for support from the Air Force, the accuracy with

Left : monitors of the US Navy's River Assault Squadrons 91 and 92 played an important part in the war in the Mekong Delta.
Right : ARVN troops of the 7th Regiment come to the relief of the beleaguered garrison of Bau Bang, assisted by Bell UH-1 'Huey' helicopters of the US Army.
Below : captured VC guerrillas are flown to headquarters for interrogation by Intelligence personnel in February 1965.

which the USAF pilots managed to deliver their ordnance left much to be desired. Service rivalry notwithstanding, it was often felt by the infantry that the Air Force could be more dangerous than the enemy.

So, with the Air Force, as in so many other facets of the military escalation of the war, the objective was to perfect new techniques, study new programs, and devise new strategies and tactics. The United States Government and forces simply assumed that in achieving those objectives the defeat of the Communists would follow.

The only possible response of the North Vietnamese government to intervention by the United States was to initiate its own full-scale involvement in the war. The Vietnamese Peoples Army, known to the Americans as the North Vietnamese Army, joined the guerrillas in the South. From the arrival of the first American troops the North Vietnamese had begun to take an open role in the war. In November 1965 the first set battle between American and NVA troops took place five miles from the Cambodian border. In line with the pattern that would be followed throughout the war, both the United States and North Vietnam claimed victory and the inflicting of many casualties on the 'enemy.' General Westmoreland expressed confidence in the strategy that as troop numbers rose the United States would primarily undertake the the combat role against the NVA,

leaving the ARVN free to protect the people from the Viet Cong. By October 1966 North Vietnam had no less than three infantry divisions in the South, along with some 67,000 hard-core VC troops and more than 200,000 militia and support personnel.

Throughout 1966 and 1967 the United States was committed to a war of attrition against the Communists. There were no defined front lines but by late 1967 the war effort had begun to bog down with neither side gaining anything but an ever-increasing casualty list. It seemed obvious that a confrontation of some magnitude was bound to occur. General Giap, who had continued to be the driving force behind the North Vietnamese military strength, believed he could see a situation where he could re-create another Dien Bien Phu. If he were able to defeat a large American force, the United States would be forced to review its policies and direction in South Vietnam. It might even lead to the same conditions which had affected the French after Dien Bien Phu. The location on which Giap focussed his attention as 1967 drew to a close was the US Marine base at Khe Sanh. However, that was not the only military venture with which the NVA/VC would greet the new year of 1968.

Below and below right: US Navy UH-1 helicopters in action over the Mekong Delta in 1967.
Bottom right: ARVNs board UH-1s.

Below: a gun crew of Battery A, 319th Artillery Regiment, fire their 105mm howitzer in support of an infantry sweep-and-search mission.

The Tet Offensive

The Tet offensive of 1968 comprised two major offensives. The first was the Battle for Khe Sanh, which began before the Tet Offensive and would continue until after Tet was over. The second was the full-scale assault on all major cities in South Vietnam. Contrary to many reports at the time, the offensive, which was considered the last-gasp effort of the NVA/VC in the war, did not really come as a great surprise. American Intelligence and the command in Southeast Asia knew that something big was in the wind. It was the extent and the ferocity of the offensive that would catch the Americans and South Vietnamese off guard.

In October 1967 General Giap told his troops that a glorious victory would soon be theirs. Although the United States Intelligence community had grown accustomed to the rhetoric that was constantly used by the leaders in North Vietnam, Giap's speech had a ring of confidence and authenticity. In fact the speech indicated that the Communist leaders were about to attempt another Dien Bien Phu somewhere in the northern provinces, most likely Quang Tri Province which

Left and above left: US troops check the craters caused by B-52 bomber strikes for VC casualties. Far left: USAF F-100 Super Sabres drop their bombs onto VC targets. Above: supplies are unloaded from a USAF Lockheed C-130 Hercules.

bordered the DMZ.

Giap's plans called for increased offensive actions by smaller units against all regions of South Vietnam to assist in the northern province. No place was to be considered safe or remote from the war. His strategy was to spread American and South Vietnamese forces so thin that they would be unable to withstand his primary attack.

It must be remembered that although the French were defeated at Dien Bien Phu, they had not been so crippled that they could not continue the war. The key to the defeat had been that the French people lost the will to support continued fighting in Southeast Asia. The French were disillusioned with the events that had taken place and were no longer prepared to make sacrifices for Vietnam.

Giap believed that the time was right to exercise that strategy once again. A peace movement was growing among radicals in the United States and the Government was divided into those who supported the war and those who opposed it. News reports in the States were often contradictory and some newsmen were questioning

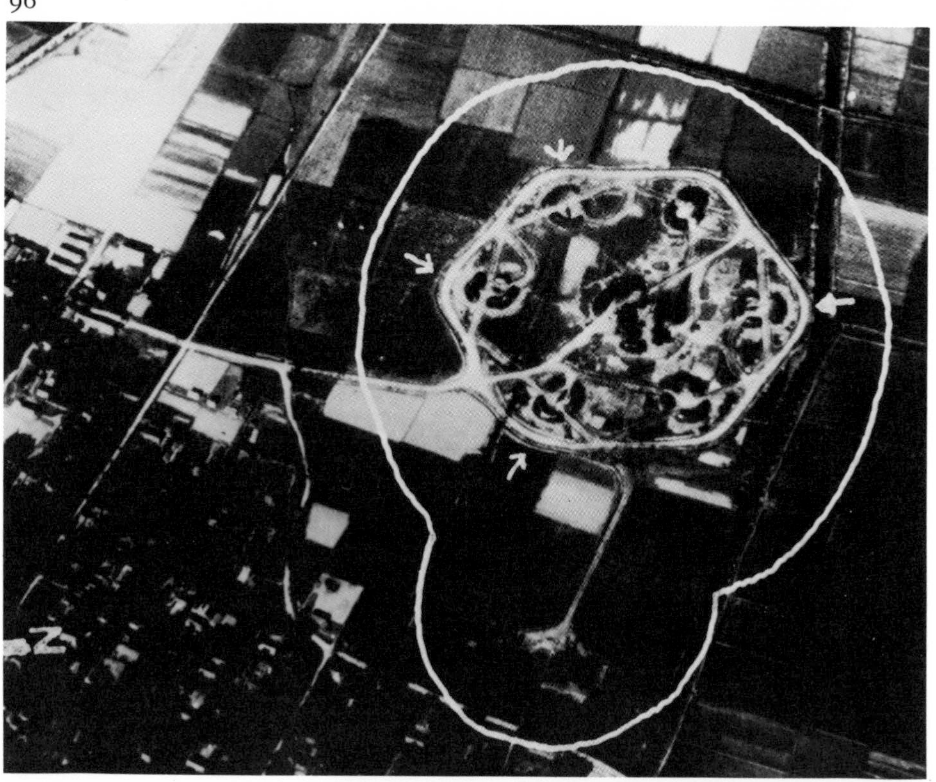

American progress and statistics in South Vietnam. Others were questioning whether the country could be pacified, or if the bombings of the North were accomplishing anything positive.

Secretary of Defense MacNamara had reduced the war into graphs and figures which illustrated that the United States was making progress. He also assured the American people that the South Vietnamese were becoming better soldiers and that it was only a matter of time before the pressure would be felt and the Communists would seek peace. Regardless of the claims, the routine of fighting in Vietnam had changed very little.

Left: a North Vietnamese surface-to-air missile site protects the important port of Haiphong.
Below: the impressive result of an air strike on oil tanks at Hanoi.
Right: Navy A-7 Corsair IIs bomb the Hai Duong Bridge in January 1967.

The South Vietnamese and Americans continued to control the major cities and the NVA/VC continued to control the countryside. Day-to-day operations failed to bring any new successes and overall the war was beginning to settle into a rut of routine frustration where the ultimate answers and solutions were always just outside the grasp of the American military.

A false sense of security was encouraged. Intelligence reports were doctored on Defense Department orders and any American achievement was made to look better than it really was. The 1968 Presidential election campaign was in progress and it was hoped that by doctoring the figures the critics and those who were using the war for political reasons would be hushed. One example of this was that Intelligence reports released to the public showed half as many NVA/VC troops in South Vietnam as were reported in official CIA files. The juggling of figures on all aspects of the war to suit the need was MacNamara's method of showing 'productivity.' It was as if he believed that by a show of 'net profits and gains' he could convince the American government to invest more money, time and lives into the business of killing the Communists.

In spite of the reports and the claims, the NVA/VC prepared for and launched their Tet Offensive of 1968 with the besieging of the base at Khe Sanh. Since its original days as a Special Forces Camp, the Marines had taken over the base at Khe Sanh and had created a major fortification and fire-support base in the western half of Quang Tri Province only a few miles from the Laotian border. The importance of Khe Sanh lay in the fact that it could keep a careful watch on the Ho Chi Minh Trail just across the border and could bring its artillery to bear on that supply route. Khe Sanh was definitely an irritation to the NVA and if it could be taken it would not only be a great victory for the North, but would eliminate one of the key United States installations for monitoring the trail.

When the Marines arrived in 1967 the Green Berets moved their own camp closer to the Laotian border, near the Montagnard village of Lang Vei. The Montagnards, or 'Mountain Yards' as the word was often pronounced by the Americans, were a people who inhabited the area along the South Vietnamese and Laotian border. They felt no real love for the Laotians or the Vietnamese and for many years had been considered a second-class minority in Vietnam. Until the Special Forces convinced them to channel their hostilities against the Communists, they were active against any Vietnamese outsider who came into their territories.

It is difficult to understand precisely why it happened, but the Montagnards were extremely receptive to the Green Beret/Special Forces advisors throughout the American involvement in Vietnam. Perhaps it was because the Special Forces personnel, who were the first members of the American combat forces who came into close personal contact with the South Vietnamese people, could see a formidable ally in the 'Yards.'

The honesty and sense of honor of the Montagnard was beyond reproach. I personally know of an incident in which an American advisor accidentally left his wedding ring in a Montagnard village and had resigned himself to its loss. A Montagnard boy found the ring and after four weeks of tracking located the advisor and delivered the ring to him. Without a word the boy turned and started back to his village. On contact I found the Montagnards to be a reserved though warm and generous people, but I know from experience that they could be equally vicious. The worst atrocity I witnessed in Vietnam was perpetrated by the Montagnards against a VC soldier. That soldier was found tied to a tree and tortured in a gruesome manner. I later learned that he and several other VC troops had been caught after raping a young Montagnard girl and had been 'appropriately' punished. As long as the American advisor was straightforward and completely honest with the Montagnards, he had allies who were perhaps without equal as fighting men in Vietnam. Their primary weapons were usually nothing more than their small hand-made crossbows, but they were amazingly accurate and deadly with that weapon.

Although the Special Forces and Marines had secured the area around Khe Sanh by December 1967, in-

Below: troops of the 38th Ranger Battalion close in on a VC position in the Cholon suburb of Saigon in the aftermath of the Tet offensive.
Right: UH-1 'Hueys' move troops of 1st Air Cavalry Division (Airmobile) into the Bong Song District during Operation 'White Wing,' February 1966.
Below right: a UH-1B of the 179th Aviation Company, US Army, lifts off.

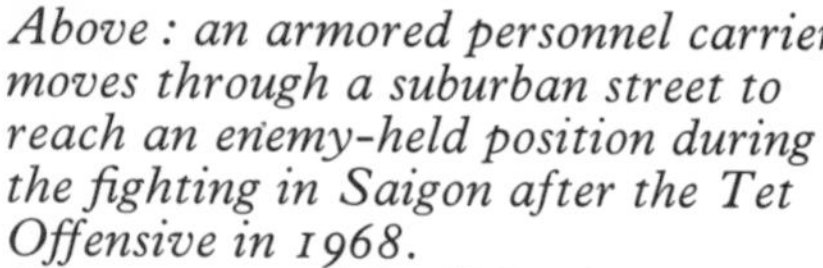

Above : an armored personnel carrier moves through a suburban street to reach an enemy-held position during the fighting in Saigon after the Tet Offensive in 1968.
Top : troops of the US 9th Infantry Division fire on North Vietnamese Army positions south of the 'Y' bridge in Saigon, May 1968.

Above right : Hue residents begin sifting through the wreckage of their homes in February 1968, as ARVN troops finally win the 25-day battle for Vietnam's ancient capital.
Right : American and South Vietnamese troops fight to retake a BOQ on the outskirts of Saigon during the Tet offensive in February 1968.

creased enemy activity was being detected. Early reports indicated that two NVA divisions were operating in the area. They were later identified as the 325th and 304th Divisions which had gained fame at the Battle of Dien Bien Phu 13 years earlier. Another NVA division was located northeast of Khe Sanh at a vantage site known as the Rock Pile on Route 9. From that position it would act as a block to cut off United States troops' movements from Quang Tri and Dong Ha while the other NVA divisions applied their strengths against Khe Sanh.

The Americans had chosen to fortify a valley position which was surrounded by hills, as had the French at Dien Bien Phu. Giap's strategy was for the surrounding hills to be assaulted and taken then used as an NVA artillery position. The Special Forces position at Lang Vei was to be cut off and eliminated while the main fire-support base at Khe Sanh would be weakened and finally assaulted.

Along with the obvious similarity between Khe Sanh and Dien Bien Phu the location of the Marine base appealed to Giap. Khe Sanh was only 14 miles from the DMZ and six miles from the Laotian section of the Ho Chi Minh Trail. Giap could therefore place his long-range artillery in the safety of the DMZ and supplies and reinforcements would only be a few miles away.

Giap had apparently considered every possible aspect of the intended battle except one. He failed to give adequate recognition to the ability of the American forces to resupply by air. He intended to stop all resupply operations by positioning antiaircraft artillery on the hills around Khe Sanh, but apparently he did not realize that the means and methods of air support had made great strides in the years since Dien Bien Phu. Khe Sanh would not be the easy victory he had hoped it would be.

The siege at Khe Sanh began on 21 January 1968, only six days after the bombing halt of Haiphong, North Vietnam's main port, and three days after the bombing halt of Hanoi in preparation for another Tet Holiday Truce. It would soon become evident that the North intended more than the elimination of a key fire support base. Ten days after the initial attack on Khe Sanh, while the Americans and South Vietnamese were concentrating on that sector, the Tet Offensive would begin.

Just before dawn on 21 January the Communist attack was launched against Khe Sanh. Although it inflicted few casualties, it destroyed the main supply dump and several helicopters. The remainder of the day was

spent in probing attacks on the Marine garrisons holding the outer hills around Khe Sanh and against the Special Forces camp at Lang Vei. With reports confirming that a major battle was imminent, the Marine commander, Colonel David Lownds, took action to protect and evacuate the Vietnamese civilians in the village of Khe Sanh. Running skirmishes took place as the Marines gathered the villagers into the protection of the base so that they could be flown to the safety of Da Nang or Quang Tri. The Marines also tried to keep the road between themselves and Lang Vei open. The number of troops at the Special Forces camp had recently increased due to the destruction of a Royal Laotion border outpost, overrun earlier in the month, as the survivors had taken refuge at Lang Vei.

Immediate reinforcements were flown into Khe Sanh and 1500 men joined the defenders, but the main concern was for replacing ammunition and supplies. Air Force cargo planes and Army helicopters flew continuous missions through heavy fire to deliver those supplies on 22 January.

On 23 January the NVA began to close the ring around Khe Sanh. Intelligence sources estimated that 18,000 NVA regular combat troops were gathered to attack the base. Over the next two days the weather changed and the entire western half of Quang Tri Province and parts of Laos were enveloped in a thick blanket of fog. This was exactly what Giap needed. He had found it difficult to hinder the flow of supplies from the air and had suffered from the USAF's close air support. He initiated a heavy bombardment of the base and NVA troops advanced under the cover of the fog to within 1000 meters of the airstrip. They dug themselves in and used those positions not only to send mortar fire onto the air strip but as a base for their final assault.

On 26 January every available American aircraft flew missions in support of the besieged base. Khe Sanh was given top priority and more than 450 missions were flown on that day alone. Antiaircraft defenses had been improved by the NVA while the fog had covered the area and many of the missions were forced to abort. Nevertheless, more and more aircraft kept dropping their ordnance on what they thought were enemy positions in the hope of crippling the NVA attack. In conjunction with those attacks ARVN Rangers were flown in to reinforce the garrison. They were elite troops and were reputed to be the best fighters in the ARVN ranks. These men had been given two orders by the South Vietnamese command; to fill in any gaps in the defenses and stop any breakthrough which may occur; and to fight to the last man if the base was overrun.

Other troops in Quang Tri Province were locked in battle trying to reopen Route 9 so that they could bring supplies and reinforcements through to Khe Sanh. This effort could become important if the weather took a pro-

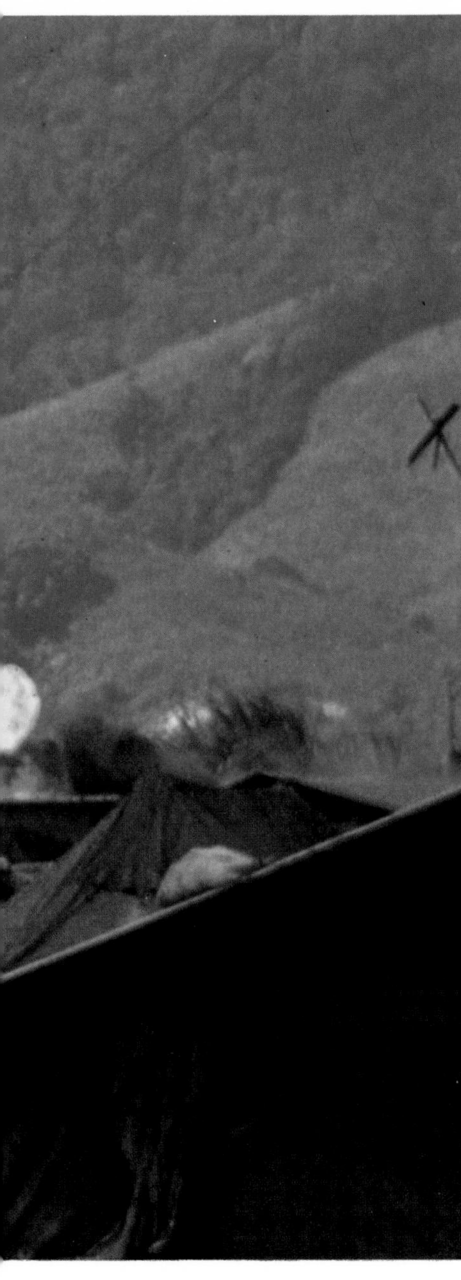

Above left: smoke rises from a blazing fuel dump at Khe Sanh.

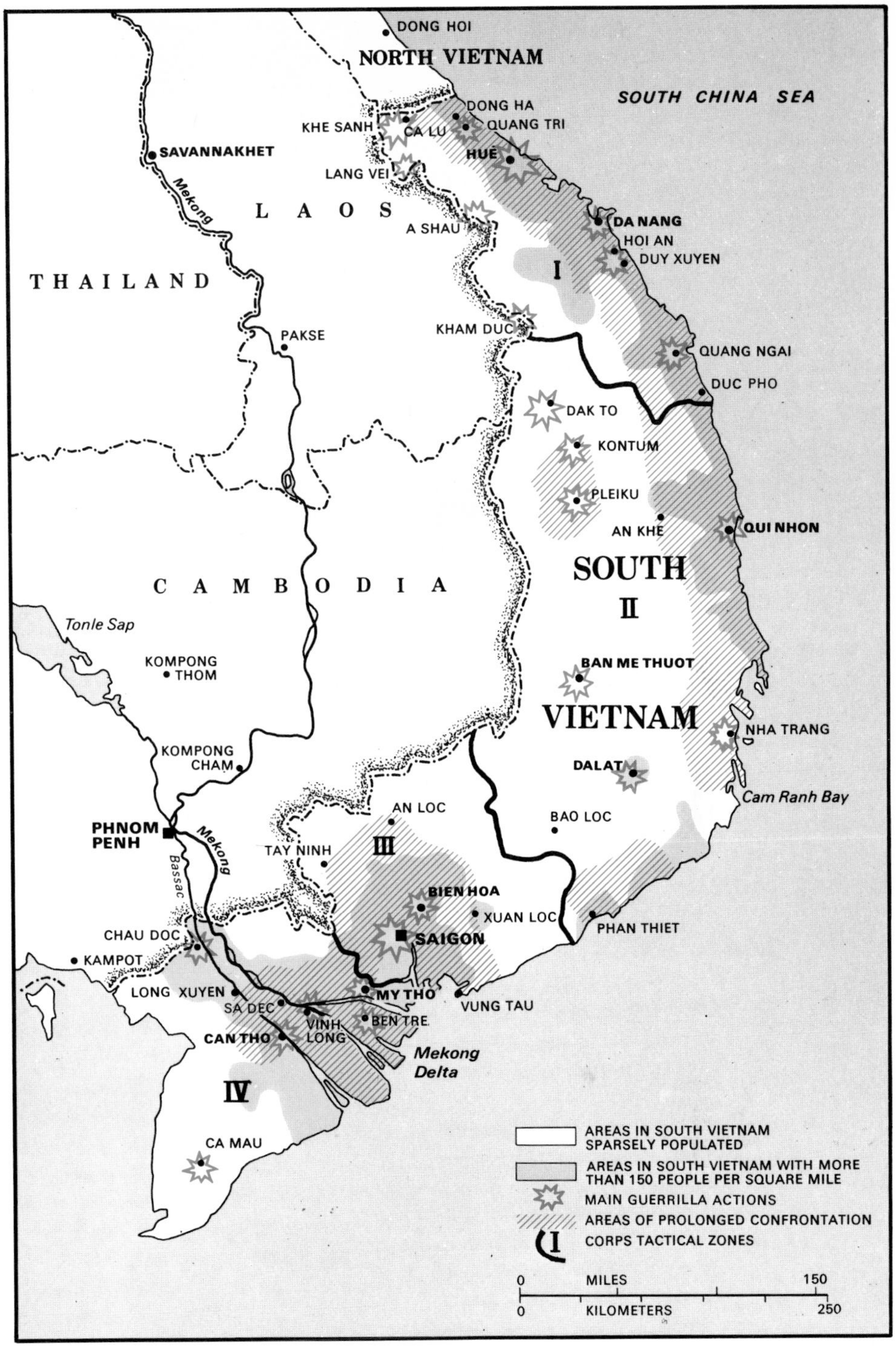

Above: a map of South Vietnam at the time of the Tet Offensive, 1968.

longed turn for the worse and aircraft missions were drastically reduced. The buildup of NVA troops had reached proportions that alarmed the military command. It is estimated that more than 50,000 NVA regulars were besieging Khe Sanh and had isolated all other support bases in the northern area of Quang Tri Province.

All attention was focused on the siege. Many in South Vietnam believed that Khe Sanh was the battle that would ultimately decide the war and that the enemy would risk everything in hopes of defeating the Americans. However General Westmoreland was not convinced that this was the only front. Although the Christmas and Tet Truce was not observed in the five northern provinces of South Vietnam, it did exist elsewhere. The lull in enemy activity bothered the general. Although Westmoreland still believed that Khe Sanh was the keystone of the offensive, he also believed that the enemy would take advantage of the truce and the situation in other areas. At any time they could launch an assault elsewhere that would tie down American troops, so that they could not reinforce Khe Sanh. The question Westmoreland could not answer was where such attacks might come and if they came how strong they would be. All reports seemed to indicate that the NVA/VC had committed everything they had to the battle at Khe Sanh. Westmoreland did not have long to wait for the answer to his questions.

On the morning of 30 January the Tet Offensive of 1968 began to unfold. What came as a surprise to the Americans and South Vietnamese was that the great offensive was not concentrated just on winning at Khe Sanh or attacking other bases in that area. NVA/VC troops struck in force against all major cities and villages of South Vietnam, from the northernmost city of Dong Ha to the Mekong Delta and Ca Mau. The main thrusts of the offensive were aimed at two primary targets; the capital city Saigon and the ancient capital Hue. The Americans were also surprised that the attacks were so well organized and coordinated and made by NVA and VC regulars. Although in many places their attacks were small and easily beaten back, each one showed evidence of having been well thought out and executed. The offensive was obviously not launched on the spur of the moment or on a whim from Hanoi.

In Saigon the attack began at 0300 hours and was launched by some 5000 troops who had infiltrated the city in the weeks prior to the offensive. They had managed to enter Saigon disguised as peasants arriving in the capital to celebrate the Tet Holiday with friends and relatives and carried no weapons, or any other objects which could betray them. Weapons and uniforms were smuggled in separately in laundry trucks, by vendors and even through staging bogus funerals for South Vietnamese soldiers. Once inside the city the troops assembled in predetermined areas to form their units and be issued with their equipment. The preparations were managed so well that no one suspected. One NVA soldier revealed under interrogation after the offensive that many units test fired their weapons in the evenings during fireworks displays.

When the attack began, Saigon was taken completely by surprise. The entire city came under attack simultaneously. The soldiers were so sure of their victory that they were not afraid to dress in their NVA uniforms. The initial targets were the National Police and American MPs who were cruising through the streets on their nightly rounds. How these masses of armed troops escaped the notice of those policing units remains a mystery, as most of the police on duty that night were killed.

More than 700 men attacked Tan Son Nhut airfield and the adjacent MACV compound to destroy the command post of the Seventh Air Force. Surprise was so complete that the entire force slipped through without the alarm being raised. In fact, NVA/VC troops came to within 1000 yards of their objective before being challenged. The fighting at Tan Son Nhut was extremely heavy and United States' casualties mounted quickly. The compounds were garrisoned almost entirely by support troops, air crewmen, and maintenance personnel, who were not accustomed to firing their weapons except on the practice ranges. The fighting became so desperate, especially on the MACV compound, that General Westmoreland had to retreat to a windowless command bunker and give the order for his staff to draw their weapons and join the defenders throughout the compound. The degree of surprise was again demonstrated by the fact that 80 percent of all troops in the compound, including Westmoreland's Staff, had to first get to the supply rooms to find weapons before they could defend themselves.

One NVA/VC suicide squad attacked Independence Palace, while other units attacked the National

Police Barracks, radio stations, army billets and any location even remotely related to the American and South Vietnamese governments. Even the headquarters of the South Vietnamese Joint General Staff was infiltrated by an NVA unit dressed as ARVN soldiers. The South Vietnamese officers had to barricade themselves in and fight a desperate defensive action until friendly troops finally came to their rescue. The majority of South Vietnamese casualties in that compound were inflicted by weapons and machine guns mounted to guard the installation, which were turned against them by the NVA/VC.

Another objective for a major attack was the United States Embassy, where 19 NVA/VC commandos wearing civilian clothing attacked and nearly overwhelmed the guard. Only five MPs were on duty that night, one more than usual. The fighting at the Embassy continued for five hours and was dubbed later as the 'Battle for Bunker's Bunker,' as the Ambassador was Ellesworth Bunker. The Embassy staff was only saved through the personal bravery of the Marine guard. They had fought the commandos to a standstill and were finally relieved when two platoons of the American 101st Airborne Division arrived to support them. Even then the situation was still considered critical and, rather than take the chance of overlooking any of the attackers, the order was given to kill anyone inside the compound who was not an American. When the battle finally ended 19 commandos, five American soldiers and two South Vietnamese chauffeurs who had been unlucky enough to be in the compound were dead.

Even as these attacks were in progress other incidents were taking place throughout the city. In one area a parade was being held in honor of the 'new liberators who had come to free the people from the corrupt puppet government of the American Imperialists.' After the parade the population was 'questioned' – using physical violence – to reveal any government officials or Americans who might live in the area. Also within the city the NVA set up summary courts where captured ARVN and American troops were tried, sentenced and executed. Those executions were done in full view of the people of Saigon, so that the population would understand exactly what happened to enemies of the Vietnamese people.

By the afternoon of 30 June President Nguyen Van Thieu had declared martial law in Saigon. By that time confusion had turned into chaos on both sides, and panic led to erratic behavior and atrocities. One incident which received the greatest amount of publicity occurred when the Chief of

Left: ARVN Rangers move through the western section of Cholon, after driving the Viet Cong out.
Below left: a helicopter gunship's rockets explode in VC-held Cholon.

Below: troops of the 3rd Battalion, 7th Infantry Regiment moves out to take up perimeter positions at Phu Thu Race Track near the Saigon suburb of Cholon, February 1968.

Above : a US Army long-range patrol team engages the enemy, September 1969.

Below : a CH-47 Chinook helicopter resupplies a fire-support base.

Right : UH-1s return from a jungle patrol to refuel at Bu Dop Camp.

the Saigon Police executed a captured VC soldier while a press photographer recorded the entire incident. The United States Command was so enraged over the incident that they ordered Thieu to stop any further reprisals, especially in front of the press. The command did not do this for humanitarian reasons, but because the American generals were afraid that the publicity would lead to the execution of United States' troops who had been taken prisoner. The command was already concerned about the missing MPs and apparently failed to realize that the NVA/VC were not taking prisoners.

The release of the photographs of the execution of the VC soldier brought a sudden awareness of the nature of the war in Vietnam to the people of the United States. For myself, who had been raised on the belief that the United States and its allies were always the 'good guys,' the reports of the execution were a crushing blow. It was a naive, view, but one which was shared by the majority of American people. The American people were confused by the incident and although the United States forces would discover evidence of mass butchery committed by the NVA/VC throughout South Vietnam, that one photograph of an atrocity by the American ally would remain uppermost in the minds of the American people. Perhaps Americans did not yet doubt they were the good guys, but they were not now quite so certain that they could say the same for our South Vietnamese allies.

By 1 February Saigon was a burning battleground. Communist positions were scattered throughout the city and United States' and ARVN troops were fighting from house to house to dislodge the enemy. American aircraft flew over the city bombing areas suspected of being enemy strongholds. The Command in Saigon soon realized that the main concentration of NVA/VC forces was in the Chinese suburb of Cholon. This did not surprise the armies or the government as the large Buddhist population in that suburb was in constant conflict with the South Vietnamese government. The NVA/VC appeared to have found allies in Cholon and attempts to flush the Communists out of the area met stiff resistance. It was also soon realized that the Cholon suburb had been the original staging area for the attack on Saigon. Because of that fact South Vietnamese officials urged that Cholon and its entire population be destroyed.

For four more days the bitter fighting in Cholon continued. Many areas which the American and ARVN troops felt they had permanently cleared were in Communist possession once again. It seemed that as they cleared an area the NVA/VC would simply move to another and the cycle would start over once more. Tan Son Nhut Airbase was again attacked and the fighting there raged for more than 36 hours. By the evening of 5 February the situation in the city was being stabilized and enemy resistance was confined solely to the Cholon sector. On 7 February United States and South Vietnamese officials began to consider that things were slowly returning to normal and once the Cholon pocket was eliminated the city would be restored to order.

Above: ARVN Rangers and South Vietnamese National Police patrol down Side Street, Saigon, in the aftermath of the NVA/VC's attack on the city during the Tet holiday.

Right: Bravo Company of 2nd Bn, 47th Infantry Regiment, engage NVA positions south of 'Y' bridge, Saigon. Below right: men of the US 9th Infantry Division fight in Cholon.

As the ground troops fought to regain Saigon, USAF B-52 bombers flew against suspected enemy concentrations 10 miles from Saigon. This was the closest to the city that the big bombers had ever ventured and although they hit their targets, Intelligence reports could only confirm 42 'kills' caused by the raids, none of which could be positively identified as Communist troops. Any rumors of NVA/VC troops concentrations, confirmed or not, were targeted.

Just as it seemed that the fighting was nearing an end, on 18 February Communist troops still holding out in Cholon began a counteroffensive within the city. National Police and MPs again took the brunt of the attack and Tan Son Nhut Airbase was attacked, though on this occasion the NVA/VC troops got no closer than the outer perimeter. The counteroffensive lost impetus quickly and by 20 February the American command reported that the end of the battle was in sight. Three days later Cholon was taken and, although skirmishing would continue on the outskirts of the city, the Tet Offensive in Saigon was over.

Intelligence reports later estimated that three NVA Divisions had supported the attack on the city and were still operating nearby, though no further offensive actions took place. The main efforts of the American and South Vietnamese forces would be applied to the massive clean-up operations within the city, not to another counteroffensive against the NVA/VC.

The second primary attack of the Tet Offensive was taking place during the same time period as the battle for Saigon. That was the battle for the ancient capital city, Hue. That offensive opened on the same day and at the same hour. The major difference was that within a matter of hours the city of Hue was completely overrun and all NVA/VC political and military objectives gained, except the Headquarters of the 3rd ARVN Division and an American advisor unit's headquarters. By the afternoon of that first day the NVA/VC had raised their flag over the Citadel of the city and had freed more than 2000 political prisoners and 400 of their own troops from the jails.

During the early stages of the Tet offensive, Communist radio broad-

Far right: two US Army CH-47 Chinook helicopters fly in to the supply-storage area at the Bu Dop Special Forces Camp during the Cambodian offensive, 15 May 1970.
Right: a Fairchild C-123 Provider sprays defoliation chemicals over the Vietnamese jungle. This controversial program was code named 'Ranch Hand.'
Below right: a Vietnamese soldier inspects the effects of a Ranch Hand sortie in February 1962.

Left: a platoon from the 3rd Bn, 7th Infantry Regiment, sweep through the deserted streets of Cholon. Above: a US Marine stands guard on the perimeter of a 3rd Marine Division compound in 1969. Right: a mortar crew of the 35th Infantry Regiment returns the fire of a VC unit which attacked Fire Base 14 near Kontum in April 1968.

casts were made throughout South Vietnam calling for the support of the the people for their 'liberators.' The broadcasts exhorted the people to rise up and overthrow the Americans and their 'puppets.' It was in Hue that the largest demonstration of support was given to the NVA/VC. Students and professors rallied to support their 'liberators' while most of the local population tried to flee the city before the Americans and South Vietnamese began their counterattack. As in Saigon, the Buddhists, who felt they had no representation in the South Vietnamese government, aligned themselves with the Communist forces.

Later in the afternoon of 30 January American Marines and South Vietnamese forces thrust their way into Hue to extract the trapped American advisors. Once that was accomplished they fell back, regrouped, and turned their attention to the task of recapturing the city. It would take several days before enough American and ARVN troops could be assembled for the counterattack. Assaults on other cities in the northern provinces were taking place and troops directed to support the action around Khe Sanh had caused a shortage of manpower in that entire area. Lieutenant General Lam, Commander of the Vietnamese forces in I Corps, and Lieutenant General Robert Cushman, I Corps' Marine commander, finally gathered sufficient troops to begin their assault on Hue. However a major problem confronted them which had not arisen in Saigon. Hue was an ancient city filled with historical and religious landmarks. It was almost sacred to the Vietnamese people, and particularly so to the Buddhists. The destruction of Hue would cause repercussions which neither the United States nor South Vietnamese Commands could afford. They planned their initial probing attacks on that basis, but it was soon realized that the only possible way they could dislodge the enemy from the city would be to destroy it.

By 3 February much of Hue had been subjected to artillery fire and bombing from American aircraft. When ground troops met stiff resistance they called for air strikes. When those strikes were over the NVA/VC who had survived converted the rubble into fortifications which had to be cleared. Ground gained in the fighting in the city was measured in inches and each city block cost dearly in American and ARVN lives. Correspondents who moved forward with the troops reported the fighting as the most intense they had ever seen in South Vietnam.

After two days fighting, the Marines were finally within reach of the Citadel. As they approached, the NVA/VC defenders destroyed the main bridge across the Perfume River, which separated the Citadel from the rest of the city. Access to the fortification was difficult and the Citadel itself was an awesome structure. Most of the walls were at least twenty feet high and 14 feet thick. Any attempt to blow a hole in such walls would be doomed to failure. That realization caused despair among the bravest American and ARVN troops, as they knew that the capture of the fortification could only be accomplished by assaulting it.

For more than four days the Marines were held on the far banks of the Perfume River. They finally managed

to cross the river in assault craft, while helicopter gunships and fighter aircraft raked and bombarded the Citadel to reduce the amount of fire being brought to bear against the assault troops. After the crossing the American forces surrounded the Citadel, isolating the NVA/VC within the fortress.

From 11–15 February South Vietnamese forces with support from the Marines fought to recapture the rest of the city. Fighting during these four days seemed even more costly in lives than the initial fighting and Hue was being reduced to rubble block by block. Many of the dead and wounded were trapped in the debris and the rats seemed to be the only creatures that continued to survive. For those who fought in Hue the stench and horrors of the corpses and the rats would never be forgotten.

On 20 February American troops assaulted the Citadel with the support of ARVN troops, rockets, napalm and gases. On 21 February the battle finally swung in the Marines' favor as the bad weather that had hampered the air support lifted, allowing combat aircraft to sight their targets and deliver their attacks with greater accuracy. By 22 February the VC held only the southwestern corner of the Citadel and on the following day even that position was finally eliminated. With the Citadel captured, those NVA/VC troops who could travel slipped out of the city under the cover of darkness. On 25 February the Battle for Hue was officially ended.

Casualties in Hue were so heavy for both sides that the Communists and the Americans each claimed victory. In conflicting reports casualty counts showed the loss of unprecedented numbers of troops. In the city alone the Communists claimed to have killed more than 1000 Americans and 1200 ARVN troops, while the United States listed 119 American and 363 South Vietnamese dead. Regardless of the claims of the opposing forces, the fact remained that more than 100,000 Vietnamese were made homeless and thousands of civilians killed. They were either shot by the 'liberators' for sympathizing with the Americans, or killed by the massive bombing raids and ground fighting. The ancient city itself had been left in ruins.

Throughout Vietnam many other cities were attacked in the Tet Offensive, though not with the ferocity that Saigon and Hue experienced. However, by mid-March all of those cities had been returned to the control of the South Vietnamese government. The Tet Offensive caused such chaos and destruction that it was difficult to imagine anyone claiming victory. Although the South Vietnamese government was still in control of the cities, hundreds of thousands of Vietnamese civilians were homeless and at least 7000 civilians were killed during the first four weeks of the offensive. The resettling of 750,000 people was a staggering problem. Thirteen of the 44 provinces of South Vietnam were thrown into such chaos that any gains in the pacification program made by the South Vietnamese and United States governments were lost. The challenge which faced the South in rebuilding and resettling would force the government to adopt new policies if it ever hoped to reestablish order.

The Communists had also paid dearly for 'Tet.' Many observers be-

Below: XXIV Corps' fire-support base on Hill 88, Thua Thiem Province, dominates the surrounding countryside.

Left: men of the 1st ARVN Division board a US Army UH-1 during fighting in the A Shau Valley in August 1968.

Above: a UH-1D drops into a clearing in the A Shau Valley with supplies for the 101st Airborne Division.

lieved it was their last massive effort and, having been repulsed, their losses were so great that they would never again be able to mount an offensive on such a scale. Even more importantly the 'liberators' had found few people in the South who truly wanted to be liberated. The lack of civilian support for the NVA/VC during Tet strengthened the South Vietnamese government's claim that the war and the hearts of the people were both being won. Tet also demonstrated that, although the guerrillas could continue to hold the countryside, American and ARVN troops were more than capable of defeating the Communists whenever they could be drawn into conventional battles.

Although those were the immediate consequences of the Tet offensive, the long-range effects were much more devastating for the United States. First, Tet caused the United States to rethink its presence in the Far East. The war had spread American military resources thin, with troops deployed in South Vietnam, South Korea and in support of NATO and other allies around the world. The *Pueblo* incident late in 1967 was a reminder that United States forces were stretched to their limits.

Tet also cost Johnson any hope of reelection in 1968. Although his health was said to be the reason for his withdrawal from the candidacy, Tet had paved the way for Richard Nixon. Nixon had been campaigning on the promise that he would find a way to wind down the war and gracefully withdraw the United States from Southeast Asia.

In that sense Giap had achieved one of his most important goals. He did not win any of the major battles, nor would he defeat the American and ARVN forces at Khe Sanh, but the American people had been made painfully aware of the war and its cost in lives. World opinion against the war increased and added to the anxiety of the American people about the legitimacy of their continued role in Vietnam. Tet laid the groundwork for the eventual withdrawal of American forces much as Dien Bien Phu had led to the end of the French colonial era.

While the Tet Offensive raged throughout South Vietnam, Khe Sanh continued to face heavy pressure, though the massive assault that many expected never came. The field commander had requested a ring of sensors around his fortified position to provide early warning of any enemy attack. More than 250 seismic sensors were laid around Khe Sanh in a 10-day period and acoustic sensors were also positioned around the base, giving the defenders the ability to eavesdrop on the enemy as well as plot his movements.

The sensors apparently proved effective when the Marines were able to detect an enemy buildup around Hill 881 South and deduce that an assault was likely to take place on 5

February. The Marine and army artillery began pounding the approaches to the hills before dawn on that day, but their assumption had been wrong and instead of Hill 881 it was Hill 861A that received the attack. The hills were side by side and the detected troop buildup around Hill 881 was a preliminary concentration before a move into an area unprotected by sensors to attack Hill 861A.

As a result of the miscalculation, the defenders were taken by surprise and it appeared as though the Marines would be thrown from the Hill. Yet their commander was able to rally his men and for more than 30 minutes they fought in desperate hand-to-hand combat with the NVA troops. As quickly as possible after it was realized that the main attack was against Hill 861A, the artillery shifted to drive back the assault. The diversionary action against Hill 881 had been repulsed by the earlier barrage and when dawn finally broke the Marines still controlled the Hills.

No further attacks of large proportion occurred until 7 February, when a large NVA force, supported by 10 light amphibious tanks, assaulted the Special Forces Camp at Lang Vei. The attack began at dusk and the 24 Green Berets, 900 Montagnards, and the Laotian troops made a concerted effort to defend their position. The problem was that, although the camp had recoilless rifles capable of dealing with the tanks, they had no antitank ammunition. Although they fought well and disabled three of the tanks, the defenders were overwhelmed at the perimeters. The Lang Vei commander radioed Khe Sanh for support, but the Marine commander was hesitant since night was approaching and an attempt to land helicopters in an enemy-held area or move against

Above: the gunner of a UH-1D keeps watch as troops of the 173rd Airborne Brigade set up a defensive perimeter near Bong Son in 1969.
Top right: M60 fixed, forward-firing machine guns are carried by a UH-1B gunship of the 120th Assault Helicopter Company.
Above right: in addition to machine-gun armament UH-1 gunships carried air-to-ground rockets. A seven-tube mounting is shown on a UH-1.

Lang Vei with ground support seemed to be courting disaster. Captain Frank Willoughby, the commander at Lang Vei, realized the situation was hopeless and called for an artillery barrage on top of his own camp. He then gave the order for his men to try to make their way to Khe Sanh or any other friendly outpost. Only Willoughby, thirteen Green Beret, and 60 Montagnards ever reached Khe Sanh.

With Lang Vei eliminated Giap began to close the noose tighter around Khe Sanh. On 8 February the NVA/VC again attacked and, although they were able at one point to overrun 50 percent of their objectives, a relief force of support aircraft and the use of American tanks managed to repulse the attack. American B-52 bombers played their role by dropping their bombs as close as 300 feet from the perimeter of the base. It would later be revealed that from the start of the battle until 15 February more than 100,000,000 pounds of napalm were dropped around Khe Sanh to drive the enemy back.

On 20 February the weather took a turn for the worse. Supply aircraft were finding it impossible to deliver their cargo and helicopters became easy prey to antiaircraft fire as they searched for landing sites within the compound. For the remainder of the

Above left: a sergeant of the 101st Airborne Division changes his socks at Landing Zone 'Sally' in 1968. Left: the Acting First Sergeant of Charlie Company, 2nd Bn, 327th Infantry collects outgoing mail. Above: a tracker dog assists men of the 25th Infantry Division during a patrol in the 'Iron Triangle' area.

month the NVA/VC seemed satisfied to keep an antiaircraft umbrella over the base to slow down the resupply effort while they dug trenches ever closer to the perimeter. When the fog lifted the Marines were amazed to see that the enemy had constructed elaborate tunnel and bunker systems almost completely around Khe Sanh.

While offensive actions around Khe Sanh decreased, other American fire support bases, including those at Dong Ha, Con Thien and Camp Carroll, were receiving periodic artillery bombardment and assaults intended more to keep them from lending support to Khe Sanh than to take those bases. At Khe Sanh Marines sent out patrols, but they were continually ambushed and casualties were high. A more effective weapon against the NVA/VC were the Marine snipers. They caused few actual casualties, but they created fear among the Communist soldiers.

As March began, the two NVA Divisions around Khe Sanh continued to close in. Cargo aircraft had become so vulnerable to the antiaircraft fire that their use was abandoned and the resupply operation was handled by helicopters, whose size and speed gave them more of an advantage. On 17 March the NVA/VC staged another assault and attempted to destroy a section of the outer perimeter. The following day a full NVA battalion launched an attack on that sector. The combat was fierce, but after more than two hours the Marines were able to repulse the assault. After that attack the Communist forces again changed their tactics and on 23 and 24 March directed a heavy bombardment against the camp. The bombardment was so fierce that it forced the Marines to stay underground until the barrage ended. They would have to weather the storm as best they could.

As the bombardment at Khe Sanh continued, the situation in the rest of South Vietnam had been sufficiently stabilized to allow a relief mission to be launched. On 1 April units of the 1st Cavalry Division (Air Mobile) began Operation Pegasus, landing troops by helicopter less than 10 miles from Khe Sanh, to link up with American and ARVN forces who were clearing Route 9 so that supplies from the east could be brought forward.

Two days later American and ARVN forces began moving the last 10 miles to Khe Sanh. They met no resistance, except that caused by artillery shelling and a mined road that had to be cleared. On 7 April the relief force entered Khe Sanh unopposed, breaking the 77-day siege. Even as the siege was lifting word was spread that negotiations were in progress between Hanoi and the United States over the possibility of a peace settlement.

On 10 April American troops reached Lang Vei and, although Khe Sanh would continue to see sporadic fighting in the weeks ahead, the death grip had been broken and there was no longer reason to fear that the base would be lost. The Battle for Khe Sanh, like the Tet Offensive, was declared a great victory for the American and South Vietnamese forces. Whether it was worth the cost was questionable. When evidence first in-

Left: a patrol from the 173rd Airborne Brigade moves back to its camp along a jungle trail.
Above: a member of the 173rd Airborne Brigade takes cover during Operation 'Greeley.'

dicated that a siege at Khe Sanh might take place, the marines were in favor of evacuating the base. This was not out of fear, but from the belief that defending the base would not achieve any beneficial purpose. The primary purpose of Khe Sanh was to monitor and bring pressure to bear on the Ho Chi Minh Trail. When the NVA/VC offensive began, those objectives were negated. Westmoreland wanted the base held because he believed that one major engagement like Khe Sanh could destroy the morale of the Communist fighting force. Added to that belief was the fact that the only time American troops seemed able to defeat the enemy was when the NVA/VC could be drawn into a conventional battle.

The viewpoints of both the Marines and Westmoreland had merit. Khe Sanh proved to Giap and the NVA/VC command that the advances in military technology made another Dien Bien Phu virtually impossible. So long as the United States had troops in Vietnam and was willing to continue the war, the set-piece battle that could win the war would not be fought. Khe Sanh and the Tet Offensive taught the NVA/VC a new respect for the American soldier, whom they had thought had no stomach for this war. Although there was disillusionment in the American ranks, the Communists did not give credit to the American soldier's stubbornness. The qualities of the American soldier were strengthened by the fact that he considered himself a winner. He took pride in the history and accomplishments of the US military and did not intend to betray that heritage in the jungles of Vietnam.

At the beginning of April 1968 the North Vietnamese Government agreed to accept Johnson's offer and to enter negotiations which would lead to a peace settlement. By 3 May it had been agreed that the negotiations would take place in Paris and by the end of May Johnson had called a halt to the bombing of the North so that the negotiations could begin.

For the remainder of 1968 preparations for the Paris Peace Negotiations were given a high priority by the United States Government. Finally on 25 January 1969 the Paris Peace Talks were officially opened. No real progress was to be made. The differing opinions and ideals and the unwillingness of all parties to make even the smallest compromise thwarted the peace efforts. The North Vietnamese government, the Viet Cong (now calling itself the National Liberation Front), the United States and South Vietnam each had their own ideas and objectives. The United States Government was almost exclusively concerned with the military aspect of Vietnam, while the North Vietnamese wanted to concentrate on political matters. The VC/NLF, which actually formed its own revolutionary government in South Vietnam in 1969, wanted everyone to adopt its Ten Point Peace Plan. Thieu's South Vietnamese Government unequivocally refused to enter any coalition with the Liberation Front.

Although a great deal can be written about the Paris Peace Talks, to the American soldiers who were fighting in Vietnam, the talks represented the hope that perhaps tomorrow the war would be over. The peace talks influenced the changing American attitude at home, but the American soldiers was more personally affected. The combat soldiers had been told that Tet and Khe Sanh were the enemy's last great offensives and that the United States had won the war. It was just taking time to arrange the final settlement. Believing what they were told, the soldiers' attitudes changed, particularly those of the infantrymen. No one wanted to be the last American soldier to die in Vietnam. Rumors spread in the United States and Vietnam and day after day it was believed that the negotiations were making progress and that the war would not go on much longer. The American people and the American troops believed this because they wanted it to be true.

From the opening of peace negotiations until the end of the war American troops in or bound for Vietnam would wait in anticipation whenever a breakthrough in the peace talks was announced. The fear of dying in Vietnam was bad enough in itself, but that nagging fear of being the last soldier killed could not be rationalized.

Another important change occurred in 1968 when General Westmoreland left his command in South Vietnam to become Army Chief of Staff in Washington, DC. General Creighton Abrams, who had served with General Patton in World War II and as Westmoreland's deputy, was made the commander of the American war effort in Vietnam. Abrams had spent a great deal of time studying all phases and aspects of the war. Whereas Westmoreland was looking for the 'one big battle,' General Abrams was much more realistic about the situation. He saw the ARVN as the key to a solution in Vietnam. If South Vietnam was ever to survive, the ARVN troops had to assume responsibility for fighting to defend their own country, rather than relying on the United States to destroy the Communists then hand the country back to the South Vietnamese. Abrams was prepared to switch the spotlight from the American troops to the ARVN soldiers. In essence he advocated a return to the original American support role.

Another point that Abrams thought required immediate change was the South Vietnamese soldiers' tendency to be defense minded. South Vietnamese officers had put themselves on a five day week, with Saturdays and Sundays free, and Abrams made it clear that this would no longer be tolerated. He called for the promotion to officer status of soldiers from the enlisted ranks who had proved themselves willing to fight and capable of

Above: members of the 173rd Airborne Brigade hit the dirt after calling in fighter support against the VC during Operation 'Junction City II.'
Left: US troops engaged in a fire fight with the VC take cover.
Above right: this member of the 2nd Bn, 60th Infantry Regiment, is plastered with mud after a fire fight in a rice paddy.

command. Approximately 6000 such men were commissioned.

Abrams updated the ARVN equipment, replacing their antiquated World War II arms with the weapons which were used by the American soldiers, primarily the M16 rifle. Abrams then attempted to change the basic tactics that were being employed. No longer would the large sweeps that Westmoreland had held dear be acceptable. The new tactics called for smaller 'hit-and-run' units to act against known enemy concentrations. Although these tactics should have been successful they soon had to be abandoned when Abrams realized that Intelligence information was not accurate enough to support the effort.

General Abrams was definitely the man of the future for the war in Vietnam. Like Secretary of Defense Clark Clifford, who succeeded MacNamara, Abrams saw the American strategy divided into three primary issues. A 'Vietnamization' program was necessary to enable the ARVN to fight their own battles, so that American troops could at last be pulled from the front line. The United States also intended to maximize its effort at the peace talks. Finally, Abrams would hound the South Vietnamese government for their reluctance to change or institute new policies. Opinions and times were changing but the attitude was clear: South Vietnam must learn to stand on its own.

This is not to say that the United States was ready or willing to abandon the South Vietnamese, but Americans were not going to continue to fight all the battles for them. For many South Vietnamese military and government officials the change in attitude came as a great shock. There was a great deal of talk about Vietnamization, but no clear understanding of what it meant. The basic principle was that South Vietnam would slowly take over all civil and all military aspects of the war. The United States had allowed the strength and capacity for independent action of the Vietnamese to erode over the years. Vietnamization meant that the South Vietnamese government had to put its own house in order if it wanted to survive. Its military and political leaders must begin to look to the common good, not individual goals as they were accustomed to doing.

For the United States, Vietnamization meant an effort to find a means to get out of the war. Just as a means had been originally found to enter the war gracefully, a way had now to be

found to withdraw honorably. Special agencies were established to aid the Vietnamization program and, though not all employed competent American advisors and personnel, the transition began to show a degree of success. One of the main problems with the Vietnamization program was the impression it gave to the American troops serving in Vietnam. For many soldiers Vietnamization meant a sharp decrease in activity with the consequent increase in boredom and frustration. Others questioned why, if Vietnamization was in progress, they were not being allowed to go home and why more men were arriving. The majority of American troops were sick of having Vietnamization hammered at them by their commanders, while they watched American soldiers die and the ARVN stumble through the new tasks they were performing.

As Vietnamization got into full swing in 1969, the North Vietnamese and the Viet Cong were also changing their strategy. The Viet Cong realized that they had to establish a legitimacy which would make them accepted on an equal footing with the South Vietnamese government at the peace talks. That legitimacy was achieved when Cuba and other Communist states recognized the National Liberation Front Provisional Government. Their position would now become one which represented a political rather than strictly military entity in Vietnam.

Another phase of the NVA/VC change in strategy was an effort to take into account and promote the American eagerness to withdraw from Vietnam. After winning the election in 1968, Republican President Nixon understood that the American people wanted to withdraw from the war. The war's popularity had diminished and each American soldier lost would become an added weight around Nixon's neck. The official policy of the Nixon Administration and the new Secretary of Defense Melvin Laird was to direct General Abrams to keep casualties to a minimum and attention off the war. The worst publicity for the war occurred in March 1969 when the My Lai Massacre incident was revealed. Allegations stated that more than two years earlier a company from Task Force Oregon in I Corps had without provocation murdered 347 South Vietnamese civilians, most of whom were women and children, in the village of My Lai. A photographer had taken pictures of the

Left: mortarmen of the 2nd Bn, 327th Infantry, fire onto enemy positions in the A Shau Valley during Operation 'Somerset Plain.' They belong to the 101st Abn Div—'The Screaming Eagles.'

Above left: men of the 2nd Squadron, 11th Armored Cavalry Regiment, return snipers' fire at Long Dinh, 1968
Left: men of the 2nd Bn, 39th Inf, use an air matress to keep their equipment dry while crossing a canal.

Above: a VC cache of rice was discovered by troops of the 173rd Airborne Brigade at Bong Son.
Overleaf: a forward air controller flies his Cessna O-1E over the Central Highlands region.

atrocity and, although at first few people actually believed it was possible, when the story was substantiated it threw American public opinion even more against the war and against the army. As with the murder of the Viet Cong soldier in Saigon, once more the camera had provided proof of an atrocity. But My Lai struck much closer to home.

Although My Lai was appalling, it most vividly demonstrated the frustration that was felt among US troops. They were trying to find the enemy and bring him to battle. Most search-and-destroy missions, such as the one from Task Force Oregon, ended in American casualties without even a sight of the enemy who caused them. Commands demanded large body counts to fulfill MacNamara's defense program. The effects of war on a man's mind, particularly such an unpredictable and uncontrollable war, can lead him to actions which would otherwise not be within his nature to commit. The Cold War and the Vietnam War during the early 1966–67 era followed the theory that 'the only good Commie is a dead Commie.' If the field commanders had reason to assume that civilians sympathized with the VC then the civilians too must be the enemy. When the incident was finally made public in 1969, My Lai served as another indication that the war was bringing the Americans nothing but grief and shame.

On 25 July 1969 the 'Nixon Doctrine' was announced. It stated that the United States would begin to limit its future economic and military aid to South Vietnam, continuing that aid only because American troops would take a less active role in the conflict. Hints were also made about future troop withdrawals. Perhaps most important, Nixon admitted that the United States would try to avoid situations like Vietnam in the future.

That statement, together with the Peace Talks, led the Viet Cong to the belief that military action might no longer be paramount. Although military actions would continue, there would be a stronger effort made to erode the political situation in South Vietnam, while maintaining pressure to keep antiwar feeling growing in the United States. In keeping with those policies, the Viet Cong would no longer devote itself to strategies of large offensive actions such as the Tet Offensive of 1968. They would return to small-scale terrorist activities to frustrate the Americans and the South Vietnamese.

In September 1969, after a period of failing health, Ho Chi Minh died. Although his own people felt a great loss, his death could not have come at a better time for the Communists. His spirit and memory became a rallying point around which the new strategy would revolve. His death inspired the Communists to an even more determined effort to win the war. Although strategies within the Viet Cong changed, NVA troop infiltration into South Vietnam was heavier than ever. Although those troops would not be used in the immediate future, a time would come and they would be ready.

Nixon had promised troop withdrawals and the first area where the US military presence was noticeably reduced was in the Mekong Delta, traditionally a Communist-controlled area. On 1 September 1969 the ARVN troops took complete responsibility for the Delta Region, although American air support would continue in the area. There were a number of American generals who disagreed with Nixon's implementation of the policy, but the doctrine had been firmly set.

On the battlefield in 1969 there were only three major confrontations, none of which had any real military effect other than keeping the war in the headlines and inflicting casualties on American and Viet Cong forces. Publicity was the NVA/VC tool to force the American Government to make concessions at the Peace Talks. One of those NVA/VC offensives came in the A Shau Valley. The fire-support base Hill 931, later known as Hamburger Hill, had no strategic value and the only purpose the battle served was to prove that both the United States and the North Vietnamese were willing to expend lives to demonstrate that they were still serious about the war. American involvement in the affairs of Vietnam, which had begun in earnest in the early 1960s, was rapidly winding down as the 1970s approached.

The Test of Vietnamization

Below: cavalrymen and troops from the 101st Airborne Division join forces against entrenched NVA/VC infantry north of Bien Hoa, 1968.

The new decade brought new hope that the war would soon be over. The year 1970 began with the introduction of a new draft lottery system. This system assigned the numbers 1–365 to the dates of the calendar drawn at random in a method similar to World War I and World War II lotteries. The idea behind the lottery was to maintain a draftable reserve of young men, but to give the illusion that the numbers of young men actually drafted were much lower. The first two years of the draft would show just how wrong the idea was. The draft lottery had a psychological effect on the growing mass feeling against the war. If a young man survived the draft, getting a high number to match his birth date, he really did not have to worry about the war at all. I remember watching that first lottery. A high number would have the same effect as a condemned man's reprieve, whereas a low number could be a death sentence. My birthdate was drawn as number 25 and the war in Vietnam was about to become very personal. Like every young American who had no desire to be drafted, which meant almost certainly that combat was your destination, I took the only smart way out and enlisted in something 'safe' – Military Intelligence.

However, my personal dilemma was of no importance to the war effort. The most important problem facing the United States was the difficulty presented by the questionable neutrality of Cambodia. The NVA/VC was known to be using Cambodia as a staging area and resupply point. United States aircraft and operations near the Cambodian border were consistently attacked by Communists using Cambodia's neutrality as a sanctuary. The government in Washington was faced with a dilemma. Abrams and other United States' generals in South Vietnam concluded that the only way Vietnamization could work was if sufficient time could be bought in which to perfect the policy. Enemy buildups had to be destroyed and the Communists thrown off balance. Not only would that give Vietnamization time to work, but it could possibly give the ARVN the advantage they needed to come into their own. Nixon's war policy was one of withdrawing United States' forces, while seeking an honorable way to get completely out of the situation.

Nixon was also faced with the Cambodian situation. The buildup there was considered critical. United States' aid, which for the past two years had been pumped into Cambodia to court American popularity, did not seem to be achieving productive results. The Communist buildup would have to be destroyed, but the South Vietnamese soldiers on their own were simply not ready for such an undertaking. There was only one answer. American troops would have to perform the operation themselves with South Vietnamese support. The NVA/VC was said to have no less than two divisions and a major headquarters located in Cambodia, plus stores of weapons, food and clothing.

On 1 May 1970 United States' forces invaded Cambodia in three sectors known as the Fish Hook, the Parrot's Beak and the Bulge. The advances had been preceded by massive B-52 bomber raids. Ground troops advanced expecting to meet heavy resistance and they were surprised when Communist troops melted away into the jungle.

On 3 May 1970, United States' forces finally met the first true resistance near Memot, but it quickly degenerated into nothing more than a skirmish. Upon entering the area, they were rewarded with the capture of a large quantity of supplies. Resistance was next met two days later at Snoul, but aircraft supporting the drive soon eliminated the opposition. On 7 May 1970 United States' troops operating in the Fish Hook area hit the jackpot when they found 'The City' just a few miles south of Snoul. 'The City' was an enormous encampment of more than 300 bunkers, 500

Below: a North American F-100 Super Sabre fighter-bomber dives onto a VC target in South Vietnam. F-100s flew most of the USAF's 'in country' close air support sorties.
Right: bombs explode on VC positions.

camouflaged huts and miles of tunnels and trenches. The site had been relinquished without a fight and at first it was believed that any supplies and weapons stored there had been dispersed. It was soon discovered, however, that nothing had been removed. At least 1,000,000 rounds of ammunition, 20 tons of explosives, 1000 small arms and 100 machine guns were captured. The commanders in the field believed they had found the NVA/VC Central Office for South Vietnam (COSVN), the main command and political headquarters for the war effort in South Vietnam. Although Saigon four days later denied that The City was anything more than a large training area, its words were not very convincing. Such a find would mean the end of operations in Cambodia and the South Vietnamese Government had made it clear they did not want the operations to cease.

Another joint United States and ARVN operation had been launched on 4 May 1970 into the Se Sam Valley. This offensive supported the original 29 April drive into the Parrot's Beak. Although these operations did not find the large caches of supplies such as had been found further up in the Fish Hook, NVA/VC forces were engaged and forced to withdraw. Operations in the Parrot's Beak were not considered quite as important as those in the Fish Hook and the operation finally ended on 22 July 1970 when the last ARVN troops in the area were pulled out. They claimed to have killed 3000 guerrillas with a loss of only 313 ARVNs. On 3 June 1970 President Nixon stated that United States' intervention in Cambodia was considered the most successful operation in the long, difficult war. By 29 June 1970 all United States'

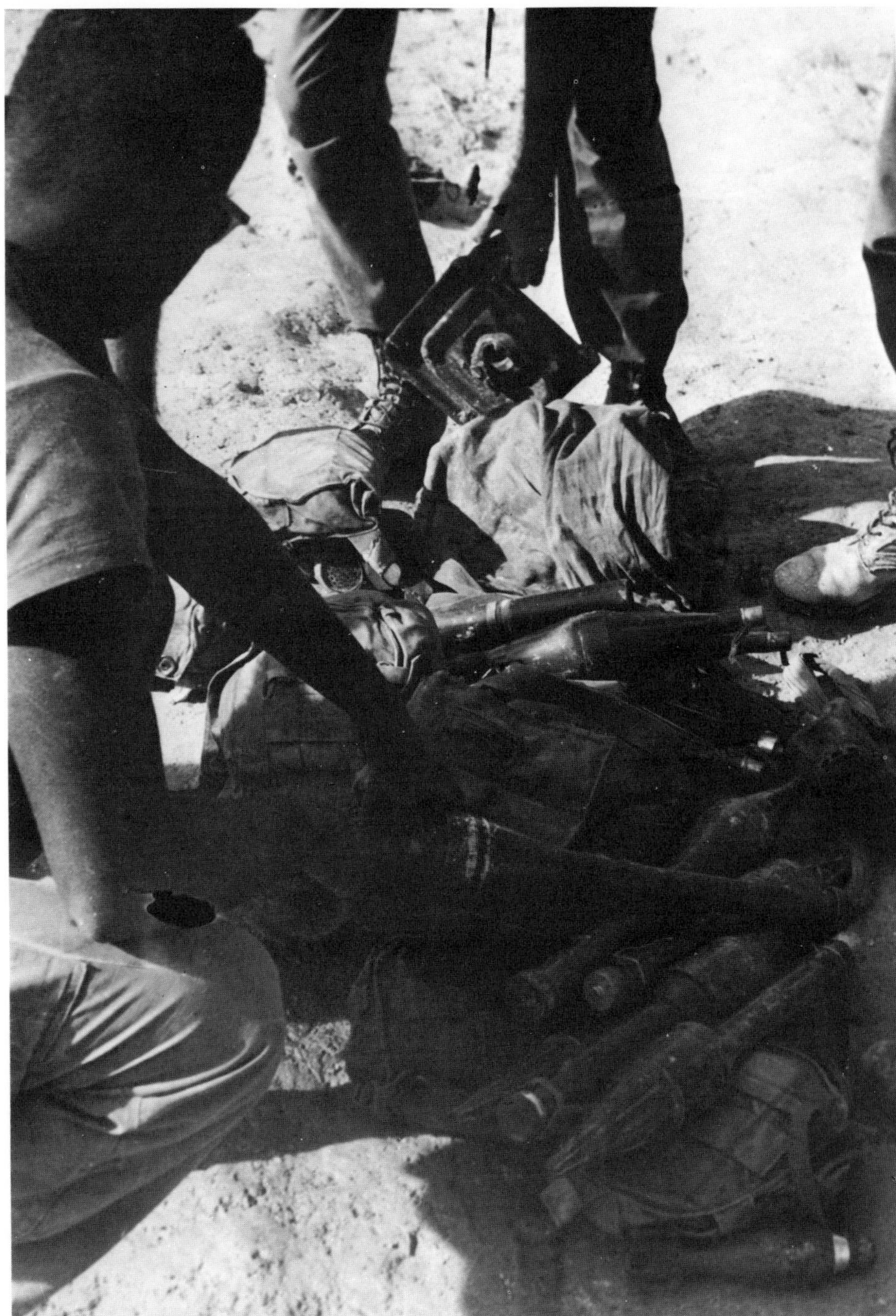

Left : a 175mm self-propelled gun is driven ashore after crossing a river at Song Bau Voi in November 1968. The gun belongs to Battery 'C' of the 3rd Battalion, 18th Artillery Regiment, which was part of the Americal Division.

Above : members of the 101st Airborne Division examine a cache of Soviet B-41 and B-40 rockets, which were captured from the Viet Cong in the A Shau Valley during Operation 'Somerset Plain.' The troops were based at Fire Base 'Berchtesgaden.'

troops were out of Cambodia and the last ARVNs returned to South Vietnam in August.

The incursion accomplished several things. On the positive side, it marked a setback to the Vietcong both in Cambodia and in the southern portion of South Vietnam. It is estimated that between 30–50 percent of the arms, equipment and supplies which the NVA/VC had to conduct the war effort in that sector had been captured or destroyed. A joint operation with the United States, the ARVN and some Cambodian troops accomplished a great deal and casualties among the enemy were considered extremely high, although the estimate included 'presumed losses' from the B-52 raids.

The operation also had many negative aspects. Cambodian officials who tried to cooperate with the United States' effort were promised much but received nothing and so lost heart and faith in the United States. This served to strengthen the position of the Communists, who were infiltrating the neutralist government. Also, senior COSVN officials in The City managed to move deeper into Cambodia as they were forewarned of their danger by agents working inside the Saigon government. Those officials escaped and the troops in their command filtered further into the Cambodian countryside, waiting only for the Americans and ARVN to leave so they could return. Once again, this confirms that operations of this type did little to restrict the enemy. Only if the United States or South Vietnamese was willing to stay in the area could they keep it from reverting to Communist control.

Even more serious was the public outcry in the United States and other parts of the world against what was viewed as an escalation of the war by

Left : an aerial view of the impact area of a B-82 15,000lb bomb, which was dropped from a C-130 Hercules to create a helicopter landing zone in dense jungle.
Below : a bomb-laden Vought A-7D Corsair II attack aircraft of the 354th TFW, which operated from Thailand toward the end of the conflict in South Vietnam.

Nixon. This outcry even forced Nixon to make a public statement that he would not send any more troops into Cambodia and that the operation had occurred only to disrupt the enemy's forces and not to turn Cambodia into another Vietnam. When public opinion forced Nixon to make this statement, the fall of Cambodia to the Communist factions was inevitable. Although on the surface Cambodia was a successful operation, in the final analysis it reaffirmed to the Communists that the United States was leaving the war and that popular opinion wanted American troops out of Vietnam as quickly as possible.

Little else took place in Vietnam for the rest of 1970, except for the usual terrorist attacks against major installations and small-unit operations against United States' and South Vietnamese troops by guerrillas. During this time two ideas were forming. On the Communist side the strategy was to remain the same, with a constant buildup of forces waiting only for the day when United States' military involvement would end. The opportunity would then present itself for a quick campaign against the South, giving the Communist forces the victory which had hitherto been denied. This buildup could be seen throughout Vietnam, but it was especially strong in four sections: the Central Highlands, the five northern provinces of South Vietnam known as I Corps Area, in Laos along the Ho Chi Minh Trail and inside the DMZ. American strategy was a reaffirmation of the Vietnamization program. American troops were kept out of combat and their losses kept as low as possible by confining action against the enemy primarily to air warfare.

By late 1970 one fact was becoming painfully clear to Americans in Vietnam, especially those who dealt closely with the Vietnamese people. Not only had the United States grown tired of the war, but so had the Vietnamese. Hatred for the Americans had grown alarmingly. As one Vietnamese said to me when I first arrived in Vietnam in late 1970, 'You have done nothing for the people but bring more and more destruction.' The programs designed to help the people were often either forgotten by the South Vietnamese Government, or corruption and graft syphoned off so much of the money that the programs were ineffective. The Vietnamese people understood all too clearly that the Americans were only there to kill Communists, caring little for what happened to the people. As long as the South Vietnamese Government was willing to kill Communists too, it could quietly engage in any other activities it desired. The Americans were there to save the people from the Communists, but there was no one to save them from the Americans.

Other events of importance did take place in 1970, but they were not of purely military significance. On 24 June 1970, only five days before United States' troops were withdrawn from Cambodia, the United States Senate repealed the Gulf of Tonkin Resolution. This meant that the United States was no longer bound militarily to the protection of South Vietnam. The repeal was prompted by the fact that all studies showed that, even with the most optimistic quotas, it could take 8–15 more years to achieve a United States' victory. Even then, when the United States left South Vietnam, experts agreed that the government would collapse.

On 21 November 1970 a United States' commando raid was launched at Son Tay POW camp in North Vietnam. The raid itself was made under the cover of one of the many bombing missions which were occurring throughout the North, but on this day the raids were only a diversionary tactic. A small, select group of Air Force and Special Forces volunteers was flown in by helicopter to attempt the release of American prisoners at Son Tay, 23 miles west of Hanoi. Accounts of the raid are stirring. The operation worked to perfection, except for one pathetic twist – there were no POWs in the camp. The Intelligence reports on which the operation was based were six months old and no one had been able to confirm that the prisoners were still there. The saddest failure of the whole operation was the fault of the military system. Many operations had been overclassified and no one person or group knew exactly what was going on. The POW raid failed because the POWs had been moved as a result of another United States' 'secret' operation – seeding the clouds over the river that passed close to the camp. The resultant heavy rain caused flooding and the prisoners had to be moved. It was a typical case of the right hand not knowing what the left hand was doing. Worse yet, from the top brass to the lowliest private, everyone knew this to be a fact.

The Nixon Administration embarked on a policy which released only those facts which showed the American war effort in a 'good' light. This was not done, as many thought, to keep the war going. It was done to keep the American people from demanding an immediate conclusion before Washington could hammer out a solution that would save face and put South Vietnam on a secure path, even if it only lasted for a short time. This was the essence of Nixon's war. Although he was constantly accused by those who were totally opposed to the war of increasing the level of fighting in Southeast Asia, Nixon's main concern was to save the honor of the United States as best he could. He did not want to be known as the President who lost the war.

The final four months of 1970 were extremely quiet. There were few American casualties. Many American troops had truly begun to believe that the war was over and they were awaiting the confirmation that would take them home. In the unit I served with, things were so quiet that we were almost tripping over each other in an effort to find something to do. There were no casualties in the group during those months. Reconnaissance flights yielded little Intelligence and the situation could lull you into the belief that the war had indeed ended. It was definitely the year of transition from war to 'peace' for the American soldier.

The new year would begin with a bang. At United States' and South Vietnamese headquarters in Da Nang, plans were being drawn up for a cooperative operation against the Ho Chi Minh Trail just across the Laotian border from Quang Tri Province. The operation would be known by two names. The United States' effort, which was supposed to be only in the support role and was not to enter Laos, was known as Dewey Canyon II. The Vietnamese code name was Lam Son (total victory) 719. The purpose of the operation was to cut the Ho Chi Minh supply line almost at its point of origin, drive into Laos all the way to Tchepone, a suspected enemy supply point, and destroy it. The success that the United States and ARVN had achieved in Cambodia caused the North Vietnamese to increase the flow along the Trail, both to make good the losses that had occurred during the invasions and also to prop up what seemed to be their weakening situation in Cambodia.

Lam Son 719 was to be conducted in four parts. The first would begin on 30 January 1971 with United States' and South Vietnamese forces clearing Route 9 from Quang Tri to the Laotian border, reestablishing the deserted

Above left: President Richard M Nixon talks to members of the 1st Infantry Division during his tour of South Vietnam in 1969.
Left: an armored personnel carrier of Troop D, 17th Cavalry Regiment, mounting a 106mm recoilless rifle, supports an infantry battalion during Operation 'Toan Thang.'

base at Khe Sanh as the main staging point for the operation. The old airstrip would be vital to resupply troops if anything should happen to cut the highway. The first phase was not considered to hold any risk at all. At worst, light resistance was expected and the main problem would not be the NVA/VC, but the mines which would have to be cleared from the road. Reconnaissance teams had been in the field for two weeks before 30 January and had positioned themselves at strategic points such as the Rock 'Pile, which was an excellent ambush site and could control Route 9.

Phase two of the operation would begin on 8 February. South Vietnamese troops would leave Khe Sanh and advance along Route 9 to Tchepone. The advance would be spearheaded by tanks, APCs and helicopters, which were to secure the area as quickly as possible and establish ARVN control of the surrounding area.

Phase three, beginning on 10 February 1971, was the consolidation phase. ARVN troops were to destroy all enemy supply dumps they found and counterattack any units which the enemy might send to disrupt the operation. This phase was to last for approximately 30 days. During this time, ARVN troops were to establish semipermanent support bases when at all possible, so that they could dominate all activity, not only at Tchepone, but all along the Ho Chi Minh Trail. The withdrawal phase would begin on or about 10 March 1971.

For the South Vietnamese part of this operation General Lam, South Vietnamese Commander of I Corps, had selected 1st ARVN Infantry Division, considered the best division in the South Vietnamese Army. Its troops were reputed to be some of the finest in the ARVN and equipment had been lavished upon them, bringing their strength higher than any other South Vietnamese division. The 1st ARVN Division was to do the bulk of the fighting and was also intended to prove that the United States' Vietnamization program was working and show the Communists that the ARVN soldier had come into his own. General Lam was extremely confident that these troops could defeat the Communists without having Americans fighting alongside them. This confidence, as would be seen, was misplaced.

Supporting the 1st Division was the 1st ARVN Armor Brigade and three battalions of the elite ARVN Rangers.

Right: a US Navy F-4 Phantom is catapulted from USS America *on 'Dixie Station' off the coast of South Vietnam in September 1970.*

Above: President Nixon and his National Security Advisor Henry Kissinger talk to Admiral John McClain, C in C Pacific Fleet.

The Rangers would retain their United States' advisors, although the United States was to keep a low profile and involve themselves as little as possible with the Vietnamese management of the operation. In reserve, there would be a brigade of South Vietnamese Marines and the 'elite' Airborne Division. The South Vietnamese Airborne Division had always been held as the country's reserve unit to be used wherever the need arose. Although in theory this was the unit's function, in reality it had always been kept near Saigon and had been used more often to bolster the government positions and subdue the Buddhists than to fight the enemy. The South Vietnam Airborne Division undoubtedly had the worst reputation of any unit in the ARVN among the South Vietnamese people. In fact, in some quarters, the Vietnamese people hated the Airborne Division more than the Viet Cong terrorists.

United States' units and advisors knew that the South Vietnamese Airborne troops were not to be trusted. There were many verified accounts of them going into Vietnamese cities and villages and literally destroying them for absolutely no reason. They terrorized the people, took what they wanted and eliminated anyone who stood in their way. They were almost totally uncontrollable and the danger that an armed confrontation might someday erupt between the Airborne and United States/ARVN units was an unspoken fear in the United States Command. With this in mind, it must be remembered that the elite Airborne Division never showed the same willingness to fight when the enemy was nearby.

On the American side, Abrams ordered Lieutenant General James W Sutherland, the new commanding general of United States' forces in I Corps and his own XXIV Corps, to support the operation. The XXIV Corps was the largest United States' military combat troop command in all of Southeast Asia and its troops were for the most part battle-seasoned veterans. In support were members of General Sutherland's staff and advisors; XXIV Corps Artillery Group; a unit of Engineers; a full combat avaiation battalion; a battalion of MPs, to keep Route 9 open from Quang Tri to Khe Sanh; two brigades of airborne infantry from 101st United States Airborne Division, who would bring along their own support artillery and aircraft; and the 11th Brigade of the 23rd United States Infantry Division. Sutherland had released the 1st Brigade of the 5th United States Infantry Division (Mechanized), who were already stationed in the Dong Ha/Quang Tri region, to add their support as needed. This American support effort would number no less than 10,000 troops and more than 2000 aircraft and 600 helicopters, all of which were only in support and not intended to do any fighting.

Before describing the operation, several key factors must be examined. The South Vietnamese commander expected the operation to be as successful as the Cambodian incursion was and also expected to meet little opposition. He believed that the enemy would fade away as he had done in Cambodia, thus allowing the operation to succeed quite easily. In secret briefings many United States' junior officers attached to the operation suggested that, as the operation was so close to North Vietnam, resistance would probably be much stronger. A full-scale counterattack against ARVN units driving into Laos could be expected. Although the command saw the possibility of this occurring, many believed that the force assembled and superior American air power would keep the balance in the ARVN's favor.

Another factor was that Intelligence gathering had been limited before the operation. For the most part enemy strength had been estimated, using reconnaissance photos and data from electronic sensors which were scattered throughout the area. Little reconnaissance had been made 'on the ground' in the area other than that done by a few United States Ranger units. Intelligence reports were mixed, with some claiming tanks in the area, while others said that if any armor was present it could only be light PT-76 reconnaissance tanks which overran Lang Vei in 1968. The troops should have little trouble from this type of armor. Immediately prior to the operation there was an unconfirmed report that a helicopter carrying members of the planning staff had been shot down in western Quang Tri Province and that a complete copy of the operational plans was missing. If this incident happened, it should have been assumed that the enemy knew exactly what was about to take place. The main problem with Intelligence was that it was not based on information gathered by the intelligence units operating in I Corps, who understood the day-to-day situation in their areas. Rather, it was based on the Intelligence reports of MACV in Saigon, which had proper accuracy and relevance for developing major strategic policies but not for those of tactical operations.

At one minute past midnight on 30 January 1971, United States' troops of the 5th Mechanized Division spearheaded the advance to retake Khe Sanh and accomplish phase one of the operation. Three battalions of Airborne Infantry from the 101st Division landed by helicopter at the abandoned base of Khe Sanh to secure the old runway and bring it into service as soon as possible. Other elements pushed out to reestablish Lang Vei as a fire-support base. Lang Vei was intended to be the westernmost point of United States' involvement. General Abrams imposed a six-day news blackout from I Corps, hoping to restrict enemy information about the operation. The American press often had a more accurate picture of what was happening and presented it to the worldwide news media and the public faster than the North could gather information on its own. By the 1970s many American servicemen believed that North Vietnam had only to read *Stars & Stripes* and listen to the international news

Below: an aerial view of part of the Ho Chi Minh Trail in Laos, showing extensive bomb cratering from USAF air strikes.

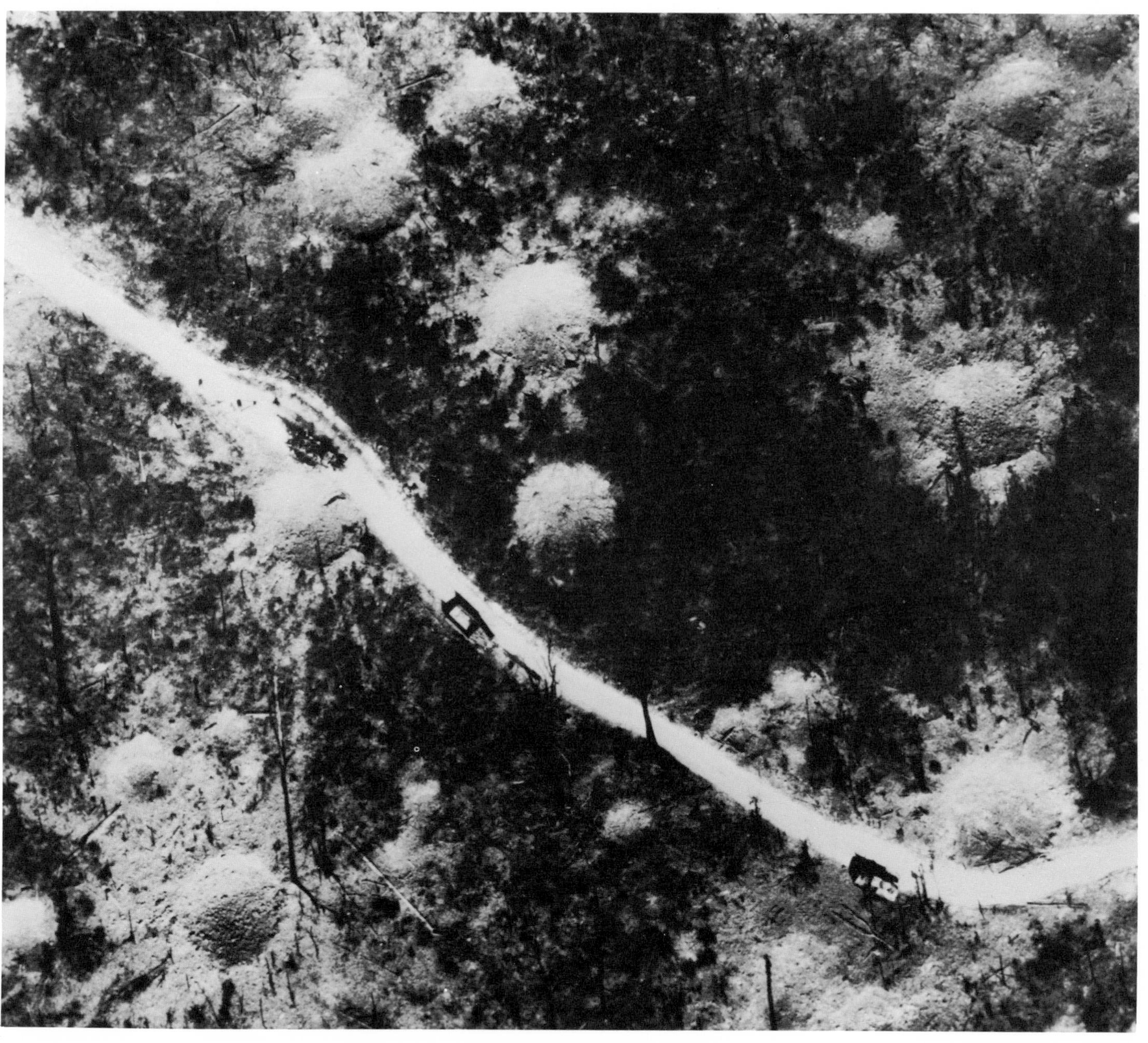

Above: a Boeing B-52 Stratofortress takes off from its base at Guam on a bombing mission over South Vietnam in 1967. The B-52D could carry up to 70,000lb of bombs.

broadcasts of American correspondents to have all the Intelligence information they needed. Abrams' blackout did little good, as the Communists had already realized an operation was in progress at I Corps due to the massive logistic and troop movement at Da Nang and in Quang Tri Province.

Phase one of the operation went much more smoothly than the Americans had expected. In fact by 1 February some ARVN troops had already made probing attacks into Laos. The base at Khe Sanh was found to be in much better condition than had been supposed. The airfield needed little repair and the first troops to get there were greeted by the familiar emblem of the 1st Cavalry (Air Mobile) which had been painted on the perforated steel-plate runway when Operation Pegasus relieved the beleaguered marines.

Thus far the operation was exceeding all hopes and expectations. Although everything was proceeding better than planned in Vietnam, elsewhere the operation was meeting with open hostility. In Moscow there was an immediate outcry against the 'imperialist agression' on the part of the United States, who was now expanding the war into Laos as it had into Cambodia the previous year. In the United States, congressmen who opposed the war, led by Senator Mike Mansfield, condemned the operation, claiming that the administration was once again escalating the war rather than winding it down. Even the Secretary General of the United

Nations expressed his disapproval of what he saw as a policy of escalating the war.

On 8 February 1971 phase two began as troops of the ARVN 1st Infantry Division, 1st Armor Brigade and Rangers moved along Route 9 into Laos, cutting across the Ho Chi Minh Trail on their way to Tchepone. On the same day both Vietnamese Rangers and troops of the 1st ARVN Division began to build fire-support bases along the route. On the following day General Lam's armor force was halfway to their objective. Again everything seemed to go according to plan, with the only problems resulting from the bad weather when fog and mud slowed the initial movement.

The North Vietnamese were still monitoring the situation very closely. Some of their leaders believed that the operation was a diversion to draw North Vietnamese troops into Laos. Then they would become engaged with South Vietnamese troops, while the main American thrust would be against the Demilitarized Zone into

Above left: a 105mm howitzer from Battery 'C,' 6th Bn, 11th Artillery Regiment, in action during Operation 'Dewey Canyon' in March 1971. It was firing from fire-support base 'Charlie 2,' 4 miles south of the Demilitarized Zone.
Top: tanks of the 2nd Bn, 34th Armored Regiment, move out in support of an infantry patrol.
Above: Duke, the scout dog of Charlie Company, 1st Bn, 52nd Infantry Regiment, detects suspicious movement in the jungle.

Above: the security of the large American air bases in South Vietnam posed many problems. This F-4C Phantom was destroyed by a VC rocket attack on Da Nang in July 1967. Perimeter guards and mobile patrols were provided by USAF police.

Right: an aerial view of part of the vast air base at Da Nang, showing the runways in the background.
Below right: USAF security police disperse along the perimeter of Tan Son Nhut AFB in response to the VC attack on 31 January 1968.

North Vietnam itself. When they were finally convinced that this was not the intent, the North Vietnamese 70B Corps was released to attack the South Vietnamese.

By 12 February the South was meeting resistance. The NVA/VC troops confined themselves to ambushing the large mechanical columns whenever possible and then attacked the newly established South Vietnamese fire-support bases. The North Vietnamese forces also began a bombardment of the supply lines at Dong Ha, which was the junction for supplies moving along Route 9 to Khe Sanh. On 15 February 1971 the ARVN command claimed that the Ho Chi Minh Trail had been severed, but that troops and supplies were still moving from the north along alternate routes further west. Little was mentioned other than that the ARVN had encountered resistance, but the operation was proceeding as planned and no major difficulties were forseen. When the attack stalled, rather than admit it, the South Vietnamese Government said they had gone far enough and President Thieu called Lam Son 719 a complete success.

On 22 February Ranger Base South was totally surrounded. Ranger Base North, its support, had been ringed by North Vietnamese antiaircraft units whose fire was so intense that neither base could be resupplied or reinforced by air. Both bases faced the imminent possibility of being captured, so the order was given for the Rangers to fight their way out. The Rangers claimed to have killed more than 600 enemy troops, but they had suffered more than 300 casualties of their own.

Three days later South Vietnamese troops encountered 20 light tanks and over 2000 NVA regular troops who tried to storm the support base known as Airborne Objective 31. This base was held by 500 troops of the elite South Vietnam Airborne unit who managed to repulse all the attacks against it. However, three days later they had to leave the base and fight their way south to join the main force of South Vietnamese troops still located on Route 9. Casualties were high for the South Vietnamese Airborne, with 120 troops, including the battalion commander, captured.

By 1 March, 1971 the entire northern flank of the operation was collapsing. Three full North Vietnamese Army divisions were moving down from the north in an attempt to cut General Lam's forces off at the border. The General had to make a decision. The weather was still changing so

frequently that close air support could not always be counted on and Lam realized that his armor forces could no longer push any closer to Tchepone. If he stayed in his position much longer, he risked being cut off. Although Thieu had claimed that the operation was a success, the troops in the field knew better and Lam felt he had to salvage something of the operation. He believed that he had enough troops and American helicopter support to set up a line of defenses to meet the threat from the North. Four days later the 1st ARVN Infantry Division was carried in by American helicopters and established three landing zones. These LZs would become propaganda sources for the NVA/VC. They claimed that the Americans and not the South Vietnamese were running these operations, as the LZs had been given American names instead of Vietnamese names. Either way, the troops had trouble maintaining their defenses.

The following day saw the first clear weather of the operation and B-52 bombers dropped their bombs on Tchepone as an anti-climax to the operation. The South Vietnamese still held to their basic operational plan and, although the consolidation phase had failed, they could still carry out the 10 March withdrawal. The clear weather also allowed an armada of 120 helicopters to carry two ARVN infantry battalions to within 4 miles of Tchepone. The South Vietnamese were to make one last attempt to attain their objective. Those troops reached Tchepone only to find it deserted.

A press conference was held at Khe Sanh on 8 March claiming that the operation had succeeded in its two main objectives of restricting infiltration and throwing Communist activity in the area into complete chaos. It was also claimed that more than 6000 NVA/VC had been killed and large quantities of supplies earmarked for guerrilla forces in the south had been seized. As this press conference was being held, troops were being evacuated from Tchepone.

On 10 March in accordance with the original operational plan, General Lam gave the orders for his troops to withdraw. He knew that the heavy rains of April were only about three weeks away and that the buildup of enemy forces was so great that a major Communist counteroffensive would come with the rains. When Lam gave this order almost all ARVN units operating in Laos were engaged with the enemy. The counteroffensive was launched on 12 March. For two days there was a running battle between South Vietnamese soldiers and the NVA who were driving them out of

Laos. What was called a withdrawal was nearly a rout. United States' helicopters that flew in to evacuate the South Vietnamese troops had to land under fire. The situation was deteriorating so rapidly that many pilots who flew in to retrieve ARVN soldiers did not know if the LZs they were heading for would hold ARVN or Communist troops when they got there.

Normally the Hueys could carry 8–12 men, but panic had gripped the South Vietnamese troops. Communist tanks were encountered at every turn. NVA regulars could sense victory and knew they had the ARVN on the run. During this exodus it was not uncommon to see a helicopter so loaded down that soldiers would be hanging from any spot they could hang onto. Many helicopters were so weighed down that to get them airborne the troops riding on the skids would actually push their feet against the ground while the helicopter strained to get into the air. In some instances the helicopters simply could not get off the ground and the only way the crews could save themselves and what troops they could carry was to fire at the swarming South Vietnamese to drive them back. This horror was compounded as men watched the helicopters take off and soldiers who could not keep a precarious grip fell to their deaths, sometimes taking others with them.

The last battle took place on 22 March, at Fire Base Alpha, which was being defended by ARVN Marines. After four hours the base had to be abandoned as it was being overwhelmed by NVA forces. Once again, the helicopters flew in to rescue the ARVN Marines. Once again, the South Vietnamese soldiers panicked and swarmed on the helicopters or clung to them so they would not be left behind. As the Communist soldiers watched the fleeing South Vietnamese hanging from the helicopters, it only added to their belief that without the Americans the ARVN soldiers were helpless.

Helicopters of the 101st Division flew their last missions into Laos to remove South Vietnamese troops on 25 March. At this point the South Vietnamese Government announced that all troops had been evacuated. Reports by helicopter crews that they had seen pockets of ARVNs still fighting to make their way to the LZs were disregarded. As it had already been officially announced that there were no more ARVNs in Laos, the aircrews must have made a mistake.

The heroism shown by the aircrews during this time was, in my opinion, almost without equal in the fighting in Vietnam. It was only through their professionalism and bravery that so many ARVN soldiers were evacuated from Laos. Going into areas that they knew were 'hot' and rescuing troops under fire took a special courage which many critics thought the American soldier did not possess. As one who observed the situation at first hand, I feel that their actions were quite definitely beyond the call of duty.

On the conclusion of Lam Son 719, both Saigon and Hanoi claimed victory. General Lam claimed the action had cost the ARVN less than 6000 dead and wounded, while killing more than twice that number of NVA/VC. Hanoi on the other hand claimed to have killed or captured more than 15,000 South Vietnamese troops including more than 200 Americans. More realistic figures have estimated that the South Vietnamese probably suffered 50 percent casualties of all the troops who entered Laos which would have been approximately 10,000 men. United States' losses, although never officially released, probably numbered between 25 and 50 men.

The true test of who wins a battle comes from examining what was accomplished. Lam Son 719's objectives were basically the same as those of the operation in Cambodia; to capture enemy supplies and equipment, to disrupt the enemy's operations and to cut off infiltration routes. Although it was true that Lam Son 719 did disrupt enemy operations in the Laotian Panhandle, it did not actually delay NVA/VC plans for much more than six months. Losses on both sides were doctored to make each look more successful and the enemy's 'defeat' more decisive. As far as the capture of supplies or equipment was concerned, Lam Son came nowhere near the quantity taken in Cambodia, although the South Vietnamese tried to inflate the figures by including items which had little if any military significance. The point that Lam Son did make was that the South Vietnamese soldiers were not yet ready or able to engage the enemy on an equal footing. The Vietnamization program was sadly lacking in many areas and now many of the ARVN's soldiers had perished in Laos. The leadership of ARVN officers was seriously questioned. Soldiers of the elite ARVN units had demonstrated that their training was inadequate, especially for confrontations with enemy armor. Lam Son 719 also showed that an overconfident command had underestimated the enemy. Worse yet, if the United States' forces had not been there to support and evacuate the South Vietnamese, the entire force in Laos would most likely have been de-

Left: a patrol from 2nd Bn, 12th Infantry Regiment, returns to fire-support base Jamie after a search-and-clear mission. The sandbagged dugouts are typical of the troops' quarters at such bases.
Above: a soldier sets a trip flare outside a defended perimeter. The VC favored night attacks against isolated US and ARVN outposts.

stroyed. This loss would have spread panic throughout the provinces, causing the Vietnamese military government to collapse. If nothing else, the invasion of Laos showed that the South Vietnamese relied too much on the Americans. The cream of the South Vietnam military, the elite soldiers and units had taken the beating in Laos and no matter how much rhetoric both the United States and South Vietnam Governments exchanged over the success of the operation, the soldiers knew what had really happened.

After the retreat from Laos, Communist troops began to take the offensive in the Northern Provinces and the Central Highlands. The NVA was increasingly active at fire-support bases just below the DMZ. Khe Sanh was evacuated in April 1971 and by 1 July many fire-support bases on the outer fringes had been abandoned. As the year drew to an end, American bombing missions increased and were aimed at the Ho Chi Minh Trail but supplies, men and materials continued to flow south at a greater rate than ever. More airstrikes were also being mounted against North Vietnam and were being met by heavier anti-aircraft fire, MiG interceptors and surface-to-air missiles.

In October South Vietnam held its

Above: venerable Douglas A-1H Skyraiders provided escorts for search-and-rescue helicopters as well as undertaking normal ground-attack missions.
Right: a crew member of a USAF rescue helicopter fires his 7.62mm minigun. This weapon was used to suppress ground fire during rescues.

elections and, without any real opposition, Thieu remained President. Discontent was increasing in the northern provinces, reminding the government that it still had an uneasy course if it was to survive. By the end of 1971, American military strength had dropped to 139,000, down from 337,000 only one year earlier. Also 10,000 troops from the South Korean Army which had fought in Vietnam since 1967 returned to their homeland. Australian and New Zealand troops were being withdrawn too. Whether or not Vietnamization was going to work, these countries were giving up the struggle in Vietnam.

The new year brought new problems. Both the United States and South Vietnam military leaders knew that the Communists were planning another large offensive. As more and more troops left Vietnam, the Communists became increasingly aggressive. For the most part the first three months of 1972 gave little hint as to when the new offensive could be expected. The only area of South Vietnam where fighting was heavier than normal was around Hue. All other sections of South Vietnam experienced only the usual level of terrorist attacks and bombings of bases and cities by the VC using Soviet-made artillery rockets. It was becoming apparent that the new Communist policy of concentrating on the disruption of the political and civilian government programs in South Vietnam was gaining ground. The insurgents had done their work well and the people were generally tired of the war, and their government's failure to accomplish programs in their interest and they were tired of the Americans. The North and other Communist factions believed that the time had come to win the war and defeat Thieu's puppet government.

On 30 March, only seven days after the Paris Peace Talks resumed, NVA/

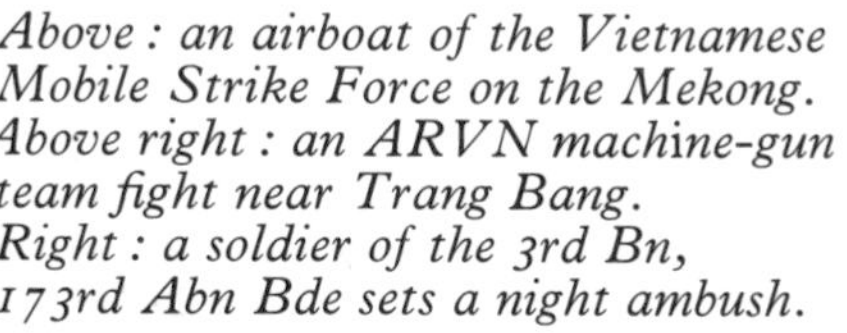

Above: an airboat of the Vietnamese Mobile Strike Force on the Mekong.
Above right: an ARVN machine-gun team fight near Trang Bang.
Right: a soldier of the 3rd Bn, 173rd Abn Bde sets a night ambush.

VC forces launched a major offensive on four fronts. The first attack would drive down from the DMZ against the support bases which protected the coastline and Route 1, the main coastal highway. Once this was accomplished, the attack would concentrate on the northernmost province's two major military installations at Dong Ha and Quang Tri. A second

Above: Vietnamese refugees are airlifted by CH-3 helicopter.
Above right: US troops await airlift to Dak To by C-7 Caribou in 1968
Right: wounded troops are loaded aboard a C-141 for evacuation to the United States.

prong of this attack would come 18 miles west of Hue with the objective of securing A-Shau Valley and eliminating all United States' bases, especially Fire Base Anne and Fire Support Base Bastogne. The offensive appeared to place little emphasis on taking Hue, but would embrace that option should the opportunity arise.

The second front would open in Binh Long Province, Cambodia, with the objective of seizing the provincial capital of An Loc and the town of Loc Ninh. This attack was also to take a firm grip on Route 13, which ultimately ran into Saigon 60 miles away. Route 13 was to be blocked at Chon Thanh to stop any South Vietnamese forces from relieving the besieged area by road from Saigon. The NVA/VC expected a great success on this front. This area had been occupied since the United States and South Vietnamese had left Cambodia and the people were considered sympathetic to the VC and very much against the South Vietnamese Government. The third front was in the Central Highlands. In early April the NVA forces, along with VC units, were to sever the two strategic roads, Route 19 and Route 14, which linked the Highlands with the coast. The town of Kontum was considered extremely important, as its capture would give the Communists complete domination of the Central Highlands.

The fourth front would be a minor front with the main thrust attempting to split Binh Dinh and Quang Ngai Provinces along the military boundaries of I Corps and II Corps. By dividing the corps at this boundary the enemy hoped to cause confusion between the commands and draw off troops from both. The main objective was to cut I Corps off completely from the rest of South Vietnam by blocking Route 1, the main north-south highway.

The initial attacks on all the major fronts were extremely successful. In some places resistance was strong but in most areas the ARVN refused to fight and fell back immediately to the main bases. In Quang Tri Province the NVA attacked with more than 15,000 troops and 100 tanks. Although the advance was halted for some time along the Qua Viet River, bad weather set in and limited the number of American air strikes. By 9 April 1972 Communist troops had crossed the river at three points and captured Dong Ha. The South Vietnamese spent the rest of April trying to reinforce their troops in Quang Tri and repulse the attack in that sector.

On 1 May a decision was made that had a deep psychological effect on all troops in the area. Washington considered the situation in the Northern Provinces too critical to permit United States' troops and advisors to remain. In agreement with that view, the ARVN commander at Quang Tri and most of his staff thought better of the situation and decided that if the Americans were leaving, so were they. As the NVA advanced, helicopters began evacuating United States troops. Brigadier General Vu Giai, who was later courtmartialled, demanded that he and his staff be evacuated also. The American reaction in Quang Tri had convinced the South Vietnamese soldiers of three things. The Americans would no longer sacrifice lives for South Vietnam if it could be avoided. The evacuation in the face of an NVA advance proved that the Americans had no faith in the ARVN and its ability to fight. It was obvious that the Americans considered that their role in the ground war in Vietnam was over.

Before the night was over, the ARVN troops realized that their commander had deserted them and panic spread rapidly among the Quang Tri defenders. ARVN troops began to flee south along Route 1, heading for the next main troop concentration at

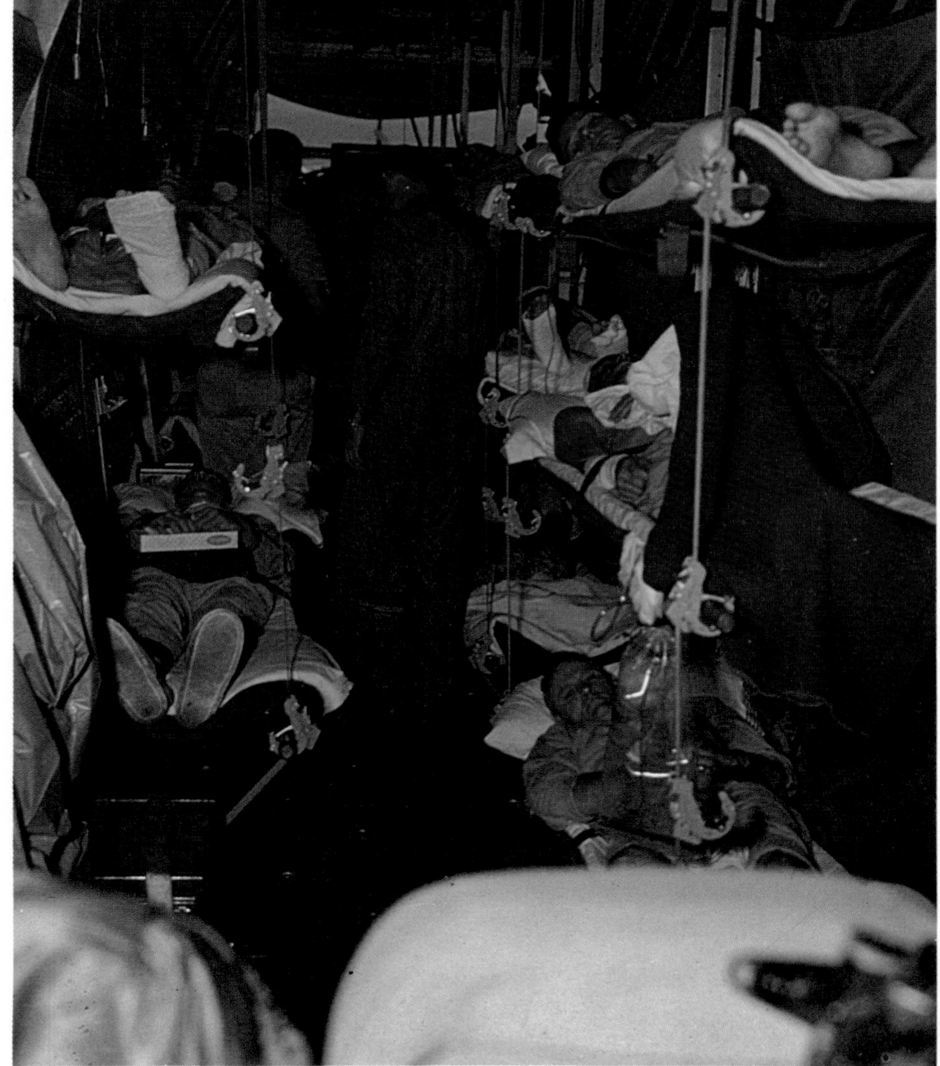

Hue. For two days the rout continued. It became common for ARVN soldiers to fight over whatever transport was available. Commanders who tried to rally their men were ignored or killed. When these troops finally reached Hue on 3 May they panicked both the civilian population and the military units defending the city as well. At that point President Thieu issued orders to restore order to the army and stop the rout at all costs. Troops were shifted from other military districts to shore up sagging morale and to show that the army was going to fight. Thieu's orders also gave the military commanders in Hue the right to shoot any soldier or officer who continued to show cowardice before the enemy.

The disaster had cost the South Vietnamese more than 25,000 casualties. Thieu blamed the debacle on cowardice, petty bickering among senior officers and staff and on a blind belief that United States' air power would destroy any enemy attack before the South Vietnamese troops themselves were engaged. This degree of dependence pointed out just how poorly the Vietnamization program had actually been implemented.

Elsewhere the fighting was equally severe. The Communist offensive from the Cambodian border had been fairly successful, but ARVN troops did slow the advance and hold the city of An Loc. Soviet supplied tanks had played

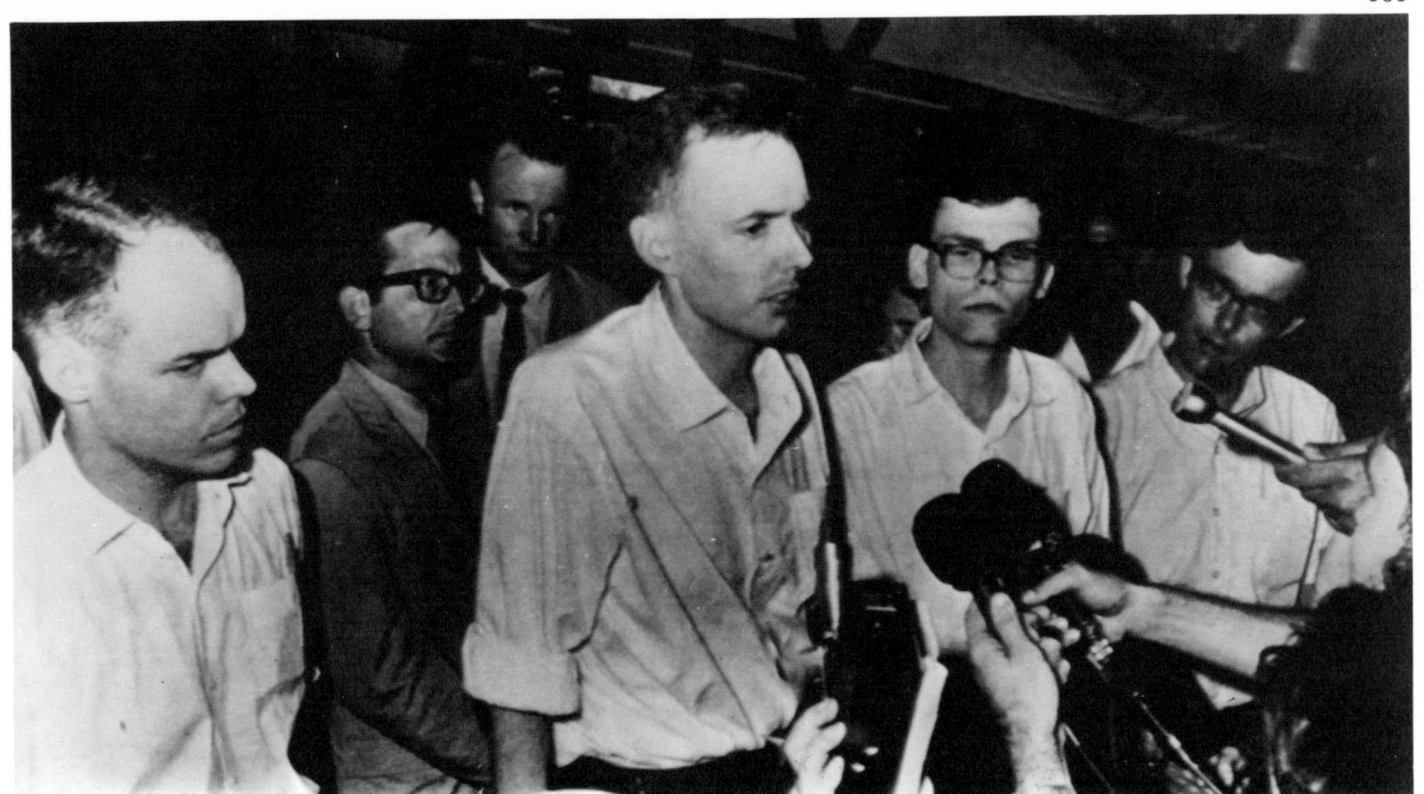

Left: jubilant personnel board a National Airlines DC-8 for return to the US from Bien Hoa in 1970. Below left: a B-52 bomber pilot shot down over Hanoi is paraded before the press by his captors. Above: American prisoners show the strain of their captivity after arrival in Vientiane, Laos.

a key role in the initial battle but ARVN troops in that area had been armed with antitank missiles which were more than a match at close range for any of the armor. Thieu gave orders that the situation was so critical that if need be the South Vietnamese units were to fight to the last man. This applied especially to the elite paratroopers who had reinforced this area. The stalemate was finally broken on 3 May when South Vietnamese forces fought their way to the besieged An Loc and opened Route 13 so that supplies and wounded could get through. At the same time B-52 bomber strikes pounded targets around An Loc and in Cambodia.

In the Central Highlands two divisions of NVA troops attacked Kontum from Laos and Cambodia. Tanks led the assault and South Vietnamese military bases were either overrun or surrounded within the first few days. Both ARVN paratroopers and South Korean troops fought desperately to keep Kontum from falling and to keep roads open so that reinforcements and supplies could be brought in. The fighting at Kontum was fierce, but the soldiers kept the roads open just long enough to allow troops and supplies through before the enemy made another attack and cut off the town.

The thrust which was to divide I Corps from II Corps did not come until 14 April. This attack was directed against South Vietnamese reserves, who broke almost immediately, throwing away their uniforms and trying to hide among the local population. The regional forces seemed to have no stomach for facing tanks. The situation was so severe in various parts of I and II Corps that neither could spare the troops to counter the enemy's actions. Only three days after fighting had begun on this front, Soviet-made tanks were rolling along Route 1, 60 miles south of Da Nang.

May was a crucial month. The Paris Peace Talks had been broken off although they would be resumed in July. On 9 May United States aircraft began mining North Vietnamese ports and the bombing in North Vietnam was some of the heaviest that had ever taken place. By 10 May martial law had been declared throughout South Vietnam. President Nixon's statement in April that United States' troop withdrawal would continue no matter what the situation had an important effect on the chaotic situation. Although Nixon used strong words concerning troop withdrawal, he pledged more air and naval support to pressure North Vietnam.

From the moment that the offensive began General Abrams had begged the administration to allow American troops to bolster the South Vietnamese. He knew that the Vietnamization program was not succeeding and that air and naval forces alone could not save the ARVN or South Vietnam. While the American military command debated, by June the Communist offensive had run out of steam. South Vietnamese troops had managed to hold key points and American bombing had taken an ever-increasing toll. Supplies to Communist troops in the field had been reduced to a mere trickle as air missions had destroyed more than 15 key bridges in the North and more than 3000 supply vehicles. Not only were supplies of food and munitions to the South disrupted but severe shortages were caused throughout North Vietnam.

Although the Paris Peace Talks resumed in July, the American air offensive did not reach its peak until mid-August, when in a three-day period more than 1000 targeted missions were flown, one quarter of which were against North Vietnam. North Vietnam and its supporters claimed that American bombers were intentionally attacking dikes to flood populated areas, causing great destruction and loss of human life. Hanoi accused the United States of conducting genocide from the air. The US military defended its actions by releasing photographs of antiaircraft posts throughout North Vietnam, which were mounted on these dikes. Nevertheless on 29 June Nixon gave the order that this type of bombing had to stop no matter what military significance it might have.

By the end of June the Nixon administration had relieved General Abrams of his command, replacing him with General Fred C Weyand. Weyand had broad experience of the war in South Vietnam beginning in

Below: a guard watches a B-52 take off from U Tapao Air Base in Thailand for a bombing mission over Vietnam in September 1972.
Right: a flight of F-105 Thunderchief fighter-bombers refuel from a Boeing KC-135 tanker en route to North Vietnam.
Below right: two bomb-laden F-4 Phantoms close with a tanker.

1966 and had also been involved in the Paris Peace Talks. His primary function in Vietnam was to coordinate and speed the American disengagement and withdrawal.

The ARVN counteroffensive to retake Quang Tri had begun in June. The operation involved more than 20,000 troops supported by B-52 bombers and with 17 naval vessels on call to support the operation with heavy bombardment. July was the month for the recovery of ground lost in the April Communist offensive. By 11 July South Vietnamese forces had reached the outskirts of Quang Tri in the face of stiff enemy resistance. Although most of the city fell by the end of July, the fighting in Quang Tri did not end until 15 September when a fortified area within the city was finally taken. This fort-like structure was defended by 600–1000 NVA/VC soldiers and had caused the ARVN enormous casualties.

A counteroffensive against Hue had recaptured most of the lost fire-support bases in that area by September. Binh Dinh Province was retaken by the ARVN and the Central Highlands and Quang Ngai Province were secured. Despite this counteroffensive the NVA/VC still had a large number of capable fighting troops. And when the ARVN troops had pulled back they filtered back into the area.

The Communist offensive of 1972 clearly demonstrated that the NVA/VC had the ability to mount coordinated attacks on several fronts in South Vietnam. It confirmed the North Vietnamese opinion that the days of the South Vietnamese Government were numbered and that, once the United States had abandoned the war, it would be a short time before the Communists would achieve victory. The Vietnamization program was a shambles, but the summer counteroffensive showed that the ARVN was a capable fighter if he was strongly motivated and well led. Finally the 1972 offensive emphasized that the Communists seemed willing to continue the war indefinately if necessary. The situation in Cambodia and Laos swung completely in favor of the Communist factions in 1972. The last of the Australian and New Zealand troops had departed by 19 May and their personnel remained in Laos, Cambodia and South Vietnam only as advisors and would not participate in a combat role. In September the South Koreans, unwilling and unable to assume the responsibility of protecting Vietnam as the United States had suggested, gave orders for the last 30,000 of their troops to be withdrawn by December. Thailand's very small contingent in South Vietnam would be reduced to all but 100 of their troops. United States' combat troops would stand down and return to the States before the end of August. By December the US troop strength in South Vietnam had been reduced to 27,000. From that point on, the only troops sent to South Vietnam to key support areas would be volunteers.

Throughout 1972 the Paris Peace Talks started and stalled several times over a multitude of disagreements on military and political questions. On 8 January 1973, the talks resumed and a positive attitude was taken by all parties. Within 10 days of that resumption Nixon ordered a halt to the bombings in North Vietnam. This meeting was the 174th session of the Paris Peace Negotiations and, although it accomplished very little in actual fact, it did lead to a peace agreement, which was initialled by representatives of the involved parties on 23 January. On the following day both sides claimed victory in Southeast Asia.

The final peace agreement was signed on 27 January before foreign ministers of the United States, the South Vietnamese Government, the North Vietnamese Government and the Peoples Revolutionary Party of South Vietnam, which was the new name of the political arm of the Viet Cong. The ceasefire came into effect on 28 January. The basic provisions of the agreement stated that once the United States withdrew its forces there would be a 60-day delay before American and allied POWs would be released. A Four Part Joint Military Mission would be formed and an international commission would supervise the transition and deal with any violations of the agreement in South Vietnam. The United States was also required to clear the mines from North Vietnam's ports. On 15 March MACV Headquarters closed down and the last US combat advisors left Tan Son Nhut airfield. The war against the United States was over, but the North Vietnamese conflict with the South Vietnamese would continue.

Above: the destroyer USS Everett F Larson *provides fire support for troops ashore in Military Region I.*
Right: a lookout watches the fall of shot from USS Oklahoma City *during a fire-support operation.*
Above right: the Ninh Binh rail and road bridge was dropped by US Navy pilots using guided bombs.

Above: a McDonnell Douglas F-4 Phantom of the USAF's 8th Tactical Fighter Wing releases a Mk 84 laser-guided bomb over its target.

The Fall of the South

Below : Australian forces were among the allied troops dispatched to Vietnam. Soldiers of the 2nd Royal Australian Regiment are pictured during a search-and-clear operation.

Although American combat involvement in Vietnam ended with the ceasefire agreement in 1973, the final collapse of South Vietnam was so directly related to the American intervention that it cannot be excluded from an account of the war. The United States considered the ceasefire, final withdrawal and prisoner exchange as the end of its involvement. Nixon claimed that a peace with honor had been achieved and that South Vietnam's integrity as a nation had been secured. Although guerrilla actions continued in many provinces, the United States clearly indicated that the fate of South Vietnam was no longer its responsibility.

The next two years saw little combat except for the persistent guerrilla actions. The Communists used this time to consolidate their hold over the territories under their control after the signing of the ceasefire. Those 'liberated' areas contained approximately five percent of the South Vietnamese population, although Communist control extended over 33 percent of the territory of South Vietnam. In their areas of control the Communist laid fuel pipelines so that they could operate east of the mountains and could supply the mechanized units that might be involved in later attacks on the coastal areas. They completed a roadway which ran from the DMZ and ended just north of Saigon and they developed an airfield complex and surface-to-air missile installation on the old airfield at Khe Sanh. No longer were their troops merely groups of ragtag guerrillas using antiquated or captured weapons. They had become an efficient fighting force, equipped with some of the latest and most sophisticated weapons from the arsenals of the Communist world.

Initially the South Vietnamese maintained an advantage over the Communist forces in the air, as numerous aircraft had been supplied by the United States before the ceasefire. But with the introduction of surface-to-air missiles and an increase in the light and heavy anti-aircraft artillery sites in the South the effectiveness of that air power had diminished. American aid to South Vietnam had dropped considerably

Above: the F-105G was specially equipped to counter enemy SAMs. This mission was code named 'Wild Weasel' by the USAF.
Right: map of the 1975 NVA attack.
Below and below right: North Vietnamese oil tanks under attack.

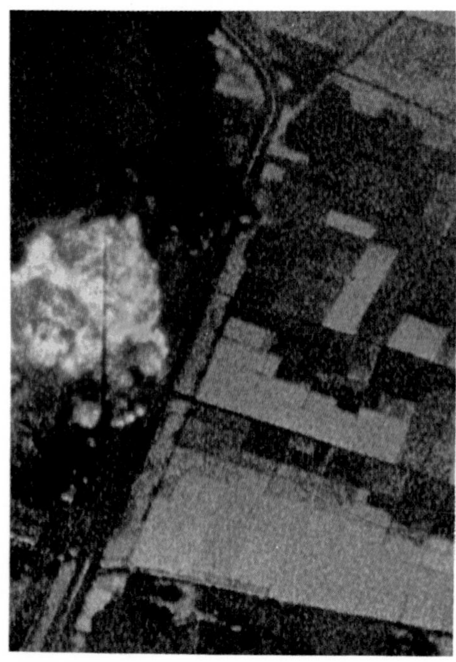

Demilitarized Zone
QUANG TRI
SAVANNAKHET
KHE SANH
HUÉ
26 March 1975
Hué falls to Communist forces
Mekong
DA NANG
30 Mar
THAILAND
TAM KY
23 Mar
SOUTH CHINA SEA
LAOS
PAKSE
QUANG NGAI
Highway 1
Central
KONTUM
Ho Chi Minh trail
PLEIKU
Highlands
QUI NHON
1 Apr
SOUTH
BATTAMBANG
CAMBODIA
TUY HOA
1 Apr
Tonle Sap
BAN ME THUOT
VIETNAM
'FISHHOOK'
NHA TRANG
DALAT
PHNOM PENH
17 Apr
Mekong
PHUOC BINH
Cam Ranh Bay
AN LOC
TAY NINH
NEAK LUONG
3 Apr
KOMPONG SOM
BIEN HOA
XUAN LOC
PHAN THIET
'PARROT'S BEAK'
SAIGON
30 April 1975
Communist forces enter Saigon
VUNG TAU
CAN THO
Mekong Delta
COMMUNIST CONTROLLED AREAS (APPROX), MID-JAN 1975
AND BY 25 MARCH
0 MILES 200
0 KILOMETERS 300

and, once the last of the POWs were released, American support activities shifted from Saigon to Thailand, leaving only a few technicians and civilian agencies to aid the South Vietnamese.

In October 1974 the United States Congress, after long consideration, appropriated only 700,000,000 dollars for the defense of South Vietnam, with strong indications that in the future this would be drastically reduced. During the height of the war effort more than 1000,000,000 dollars could be spent in two to three months for the support of South Vietnam. With Laos and Cambodia for all practical purposes under Communist control, the United States seemed to wash its hands of Southeast Asia completely.

The United States was beginning to face new problems, especially a new crisis over the economy. The extravagant expenditure of the war, especially during 1966–72, had caused inflation to grow at a steady pace. Americans were beginning to feel the pinch from the inflation which would be their legacy from Vietnam for years to come.

The 'third war' in Vietnam can be summarized very briefly as it began quickly and rolled over the country of South Vietnam with lightning speed. In December 1974 the NVA/VC planned a probing operation in the Phuoc Long Province of the Central Highlands. That attack was primarily designed to test ARVN strength and morale. On 2 January 1975 the provincial capital was put under siege and by May the entire province had fallen. During that operation South Vietnamese troops fought with a greater skill and determination than had been expected, but they were totally outclassed and for the first time outgunned by their enemy. It had revealed to the Communist forces that they had the upper hand on the battlefield. Although the United States had assured the South Vietnamese of support if the Communists attempted to take over the country, that offer had been only a token gesture. With an estimated 80 percent of American public opinion opposed to any sort of military intervention, or even any further aid to South Vietnam, such assurances were empty words.

President Thieu amazed the Americans and to some extent the rest of the world by not pressing the issue of the NVA/VC violation of the ceasefire. He let the Central Highlands fall completely into enemy hands and pulled all the ARVN troops in that area back to the coastal plains and major cities. Although many of the South Vietnamese generals opposed the action and begged him to reconsider, Thieu demanded that his orders be immediately implemented. Once the ARVN troops started to withdraw their morale collapsed, and in many cases the retreat turned to rout.

Other areas of South Vietnam were also assaulted by the NVA/VC during March 1975. Pleiku was abandoned after much heavy fighting. At Hue the elite 1st ARVN Infantry Division was not only dealt a severe defeat, but actually had one of its battalions defect to the Communist camp. Although other forces throughout the country fought bravely, they could not reverse the series of defeats. On 31 March the city of Da Nang fell to Communist forces and by 1 April Communist troops were rolling down the coastal plains toward Saigon, chasing a South Vietnamese Army that had degenerated into an armed rabble.

Although the ARVN made a stand 40 miles northeast of Saigon at Xuan Loc, the enemy pressure was too great. After fighting for six days surrounded by no less than four NVA divisions, the last resistance of the Army of the Republic of Vietnam collapsed. Even though Saigon was guarded by three divisions, they would

Below: three VC were killed by militiamen in July 1973, when a ceasefire was supposedly in force. Right: a wounded ARVN is carried to the rear at Kien Duc, 1973.

Below: this mountain-top artillery position was established by C Battery, 2nd Bn, 19th Artillery Regiment, at Landing Zone 'Coral' deep in the Central Highlands.

serve no purpose once the city was surrounded. Panic swept the Republic as most South Vietnamese tried by any means possible to flee in the face of what they believed would be mass slaughter and reprisals by the Communists.

On 3 April the United States began to evacuate children, primarily orphans and illegitimate children of mixed American and South Vietnamese parentage. President Gerald Ford announced that Operation Baby Lift would be set in motion using American military transport aircraft. Other countries around the world joined in the effort. By 15 April it was obvious that Vietnam was going to fall, but the United States Congress still refused the appropriate funds for US troops to reenter Vietnam, even to help safeguard the evacuation of American civilians.

President Thieu denounced the United States for abandoning South Vietnam in its hour of need. He attacked the Ford Administration for reneging on the assurances which had been given by President Nixon, yet when the Communist forces encircled Saigon, Thieu and his government promptly resigned and fled to the United States.

As the Communist forces closed in on the city a fleet of American helicopters arrived to carry out the final evacuation. By 29 April they had managed to evacuate 1373 civilian Americans, more than 6000 non-Americans and 1000 US Marines who had secured the landing zone. On 30 April the two-day-old government of Duong Van Minh, who had taken over as president after Thieu's resignation, gave orders for all ARVN troops to lay down their arms and surrender to the Communist forces.

On 1 May, the traditional Communist May Day holiday, Saigon and the rest of South Vietnam fell to the North Vietnamese. As the Communists entered Saigon some South Vietnamese greeted them as 'liberators.' Others paid them little attention and tried to carry on as they had while the Americans were there. Others, including ARVN troops who had thrown away their uniforms, joined in the mass looting and destruction which was taking place in different areas of the city. The 'third war' in Vietnam was over. All the symbols of South Vietnam and its government were destroyed and Saigon became Ho Chi Minh City. North and South were finally reunited.

The only incident which closely affected the United States took place on 12 May when the United States' merchant ship *Mayaguez* was seized off the Cambodian coast by Cambodian forces. Its captors presumably believed that the United States would do nothing, but within three days and at the cost of 18 American lives the merchant ship's crew had been rescued by a Marine assault team. The United States made it clear that, although it wanted nothing more to do with the countries in Southeast Asia it would not allow any country to seize United States property. Although the North Koreans had seized the US Intelligence vessel *Pueblo* shortly before the Tet Offensive of 1968 without American reprisals, the Cambodians were ill-advised to count on the same inaction. The *Mayaguez* affair and the successful recovery of the crew managed to lift the spirits of the American people.

The rapid fall of South Vietnam, the 'baby lifts,' the boat people and Vietnamese resettlement camps in the United States were the final acts of the Vietnam tragedy. The South Vietnamese people would continue to suffer the consequences of the fall of South Vietnam, but the Vietnam era had ended for the United States and the American government would do its best to see that the bleaker aspects were soon forgotten.

Above: Phnom Penh was evacuated by US Marine helicopters in April 1975. Right: an ARVN soldier weeps over the body of a comrade.

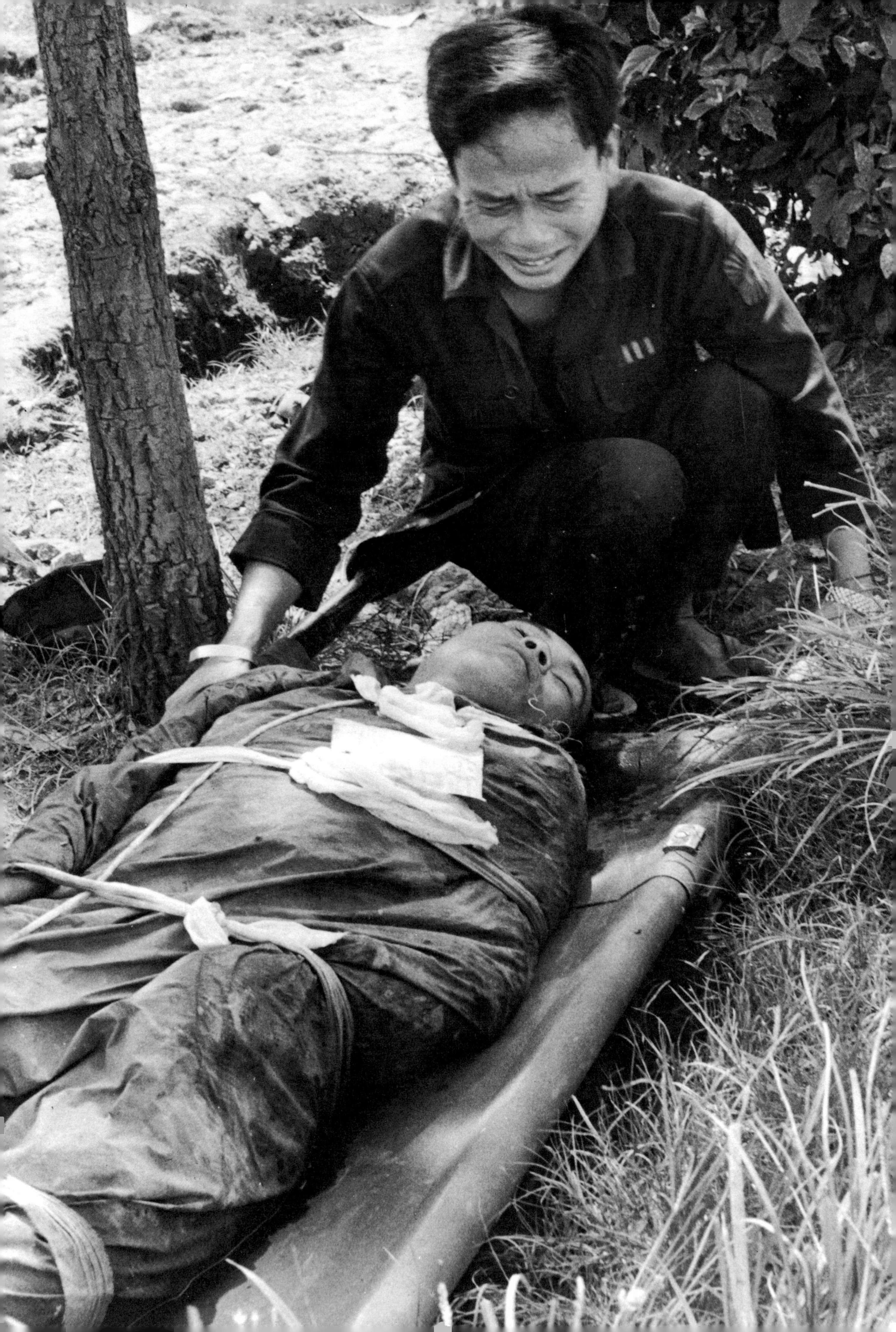

Below: a column of smoke rises from Saigon's Tan Son Nhut air base, as Marine CH-53 helicopters fly into their landing zones to pick up evacuees, 29 April 1975.

From Disillusion to Despair

The Vietnam War cannot be viewed without also discussing what was happening in the United States during the same period. Until the Gulf of Tonkin incident in 1964 and the involvement of US combat troops in 1965, few Americans paid any attention to the situation in Southeast Asia. Most people finally came to see the United States' involvement in Vietnam as an effort to stop the spread of Communism and it was assumed that, if the United States were involved and if American soldiers were there, the war must be right, just and noble.

However the 1960s was a decade of changing views. The conservative era of the 1950s and its values were being questioned. In 1964 the Free Speech Movement began on the Berkeley Campus, California. This movement began looking at issues and taking action on issues that most Americans hardly understood or which they thought had little relevance to their lives. In the early Berkeley movement young men were burning their draft cards before the rest of the society realized there even was a Vietnam, let alone if the war was right or wrong.

The Civil Rights movement was also gaining momentum in 1964. Marching, protesting, picketing and even violent eruptions were becoming more and more frequent. The war in Vietnam would have an ever-increasing effect on the black man in America. He felt exploited not only by white America in general, but by the government as well. Many blacks serving in Vietnam asked why they should be fighting for Vietnamese freedom in Southeast Asia when they did not have freedom at home.

By 1968 black American servicemen were sick of fighting what they regarded as the white man's war. The treatment they received in the army made them question whether the Communist was really the enemy. They went to Vietnam, fought side by side with white Americans – a relatively new circumstance – died or were wounded in the name of America, then returned to the United States and the same prejudice and inequality that they had faced before. It seemed that, while the black American was good enough to die equally in Vietnam, he was not good enough to live equally in the United States.

Vietnam became an issue in the 1964 Presidential election contest between Lyndon Johnson and Barry Goldwater. Goldwater's position was the more truthful. He favored a direct treatment of the military problems of the war, even if it meant the use of nuclear weapons. At the same time Johnson, realizing that the American people were not ready for such blunt talk, shied away from honest discussion while secretly looking for an excuse to commit combat troops to Vietnam. The American people were told what they wanted to hear and they believed it. Only later would the full impact of their misplaced faith be realized.

By 1965 the American people were becoming more aware of what was taking place. American soldiers were beginning to suffer high casualties due to Viet Cong action and the media widened its coverage of the war. The integrity of the South Vietnamese Government was questioned, but the United States Government continued to reassure the American people. Opinion polls indicated that one out of five Americans were beginning to question American involvement in Southeast Asia and that 16 percent of the total population actually disapproved of the United States being there at all. Another 60 percent ap-

Above: Cambodian government troops carry the body of a comrade killed in fighting along Route 7 north of Phnom Penh in August 1974.

proved of and supported President Johnson's actions, while the remaining 24 percent did not have any opinion on the subject whatsoever.

The antiwar movement was without a doubt the minority view, as every year hopes were raised by the government that 'this year would be the last' and that the war was not escalating to any degree. In 1964 there were less than 170 Americans killed in combat in Southeast Asia, but that figure rose to more than 1300 in 1965. It was obvious that the war was escalating, but most people simply did not wish to accept that fact. Students, primarily in eastern universities, demonstrated in favor of the war and the draft, calling it a patriotic duty for every American to serve.

There can be no denying that many of the young men who protested against the war were sincere in their belief that Vietnam was fundamentally wrong. It was easy to take a pro-war view while safely 'Stateside' with their college deferments keeping them from service, at least for the duration of their studies. Rapid escalation of the war meant that 1965 was probably the last year in which the war would still be viewed with a positive attitude, especially by the younger generation. Increased US activity and the bombings of North Vietnam in 1966 began to show the United States in the role of aggressor. For the first time the President's popularity began to slip in the opinion polls which assessed public support for the war. The media had a great deal to do with the way that people reacted to the war. During weeks when US action on the ground was extremely successful, or when the bombers hit targets which were of supreme importance in the North, the polls would fluctuate in favor of the war effort. People questioned whether emphasis on the war was politically motivated to divert the American people's attention from the social and racial conflicts that were gaining momentum throughout the country.

Young Americans were demonstrating in their thousands against the war. In the author's opinion their protests were not principally because they believed that the Vietnam involvement was fundamentally wrong. In most cases they had no real knowledge of the situation. It was simply because they did not want to fight and die in a war that had no relevance to their own lives. On the opposite side, Congressman Russell Long and Secretary of Defense MacNamara kept making patriotic appeals to the American people to support the war and the President. Johnson himself asked how many nations would fall to the Communist aggressor if America followed the course of those who opposed the war. He implied that to disapprove of the war was to approve of Communism.

By the end of 1966 the American people were told by MacNamara that the war effort was progressing better than had been expected and that victory and peace were near. At the same time reports were revealing that in 1966 alone more than 4800 Americans had been killed in action, almost four times the previous year's casualties. Perhaps the most startling statistic was that by the end of 1966 more American bombs had been dropped in Southeast Asia than all the bombs dropped in the Pacific Theater during World War II.

In 1967–68 the war was creating opponents at home at an enormous rate. It had cost the United States 24,000,000,000 dollars in 1967 alone and, although each day successful operations were reported, the attitude of the American people had definitely changed. Antiwar attitudes were coming from a new source, the returning veteran. Men who had been dis-

illusioned by what was happening in Vietnam were speaking out. They had experienced the frustration and felt the lack of purpose and accomplishment while serving in the war. In return for their efforts to inform the American people they were reviled and ridiculed by the government and the military authorities.

The death toll in Vietnam was rising and the number of troops needed to fight the war was increasing by tens of thousands. The Tet Offensive of 1968 and the siege of Khe Sanh caught America off guard. It was difficult for most Americans to believe that the enemy, which they had been told was being defeated, had the men, materiel and will to fight such an offensive. The media began taking an even more important part in influencing the nation's opinion of the war. With the eye witness accounts of the execution of a Viet Cong guerrilla by the Chief of the South Vietnamese National Police, Americans began to look more closely at the allies their country was supporting. It was implied by the media that Americans were not being told the whole truth. The media on the whole began to take a more critical approach to the war as it became more obvious that what they saw and what the United States Government reported were two different things. Unfortunately reporters and news networks seemed to strive for sensationalism in their coverage.

In 1968 the war gathered opponents from all sectors of the populace. Politicians, celebrities and prominent members of society began to voice their opinion along with the youth of America. Draft riots occurred on almost every major university campus and the Pentagon itself was stormed on 21 October 1968 by protestors who wanted an end to the war. Posters, slogans, and bumper-stickers appeared and antiwar demonstrators chanted 'Hell no, we won't go!' Young men burned their draft cards, others left their homes and families and fled to Canada, still others went to prison rather than fight in Vietnam.

Yet there was still a large segment of the population, the silent majority, who still supported the President and the war in spite of the doubts they may have had. America was becoming divided into two camps. The conservative element, who would use their own slogans such as 'America, love it or leave it', supported the sentiments and policies of the American Government. Members of the 'New Left' felt that America had to change drastically and concerned themselves with ending the war. They also campaigned for civil rights and personal freedom, which they felt the government was taking away.

Left: these Vietnamese refugees were airlifted from Saigon to USS Hancock during Operation Frequent Wind.

The 'rebellious activists' demonstrated in the streets during the 1968 Democratic convention in Chicago and violence followed. That fiasco and the years of war destroyed the Democrats' hopes of victory. The conservatives spoke quietly and elected Richard Nixon, a Republican who vowed to end the war with honor. Nixon would struggle with that honorable solution for four years while young men continued to die in Vietnam. In 1969 the Paris Peace Negotiations got underway and the Nixon Doctrine pledged a gradual US withdrawal from the war. Yet more significantly allegations were made about American soldiers' involvement in war crimes at My Lai. The American people were horrified at the possibility of American involvement in such an atrocity. While there had been a great deal of animosity and even violence between supporters and opponents of the war, the My Lai incident resulted in attacks on the combat veterans. But there were also those who felt sorrow and sympathy for the men who fought and died in Vietnam. In 1969 the First Moratorium Against the War was held. The widow of the late Martin Luther King and other prominent figures joined in a public display of American grief and demanded that the Government 'bring the boys home now.' The other reaction to My Lai was one of disgust and fear. Suddenly the combat veteran were to be feared and hated as 'baby killers' and 'psychotics.'

The years 1970–71 saw even more unrest as the invasions of Cambodia and Laos led many Americans to believe that, instead of the war being run down, the Government intended to spread it into the neighboring countries of Southeast Asia. Mistrust of the Government had reached such a degree, that no matter how honest the Administration tried to be, no one would believe its assurances that US involvement in Cambodia and Laos were a necessary preliminary to the United States withdrawal from Southeast Asia.

As the war wound down there was a sudden shift in the Government's approach to the antiwar movement. Social programs were implemented by the Government with a renewed vigor as a means of silencing much of the anger and hostility that was being directed against it. Perhaps one of the darkest moments of the early 1970s was the death of four college students in an antiwar demonstration at Kent State University, Ohio. It only added to the disillusionment of the American people and served to divide the nation even more deeply.

President Nixon made good his promise to withdraw American forces from Vietnam. Regardless of the state of affairs in South Vietnam, he continued to bring troops home according to schedule. In the late summer and early fall of 1972, shortly before the 1972 Presidential elections, large numbers of troops returned home with great publicity and Nixon won a resounding victory at the November polls. Finally, in 1973 the Peace Agreement was signed and the last of American troops and, finally, the prisoners of war returned to a relieved and weary nation.

America's opinion of itself had changed. No longer did it consider itself the world's policeman. In fact a pessimistic, negative attitude lingered long after the last troops returned. Americans who had supported the war condemned those who opposed it, saying that they had undermined the war effort and destroyed America's image and prestige around the world. The peace movement was accused of giving the world the impression that the United States was soft and unwilling to stand up for its beliefs. There were even those who said that the antiwar movement was Communist inspired. The simple fact that the attitudes of an educated America were changing could not be accepted. Those who opposed the war used similar arguments in reverse. They blamed the war's supporters for causing the United States to be viewed as an aggressive opportunist. They countered that the United States fought in Vietnam out of a fear of Communism and to promote capitalism rather than to uphold freedom and democracy. Although it might now be possible to get a general agreement that there was something inherently wrong with American involvement in Southeast Asia, neither group has truly made any concessions to their views and feelings about the war.

That sharp division of society was represented and to some degree exploited by the news media. As Vietnam continued and attitudes changed the media seemed to search out and sensationalize its negative aspects. In Vietnam they hunted for stories of drug addiction, alcoholism, racism, and atrocities to parade before the American public. The 1960s was a time when many Americans were genuinely searching for 'truths.' Yet it has always seemed that the media, in its quest for ratings and front page stories, distorted what was happening.

Above : refugees disembark from a Marine CH-53 helicopter aboard USS Hancock during the evacuation of Saigon in April 1975.
Above right : Marine security guards escort refugees to the processing station aboard the Hancock.

War coverage on television was a true-to-life soap-opera, seven days a week. The differences between the war and anti-war factions were displayed on the same television screens. The fact that the media represented 'truth' to the American people contributed to the divisions in society. The news media and commercial television also used sensationalism at the Vietnam veteran's expense. In too many instances the combat veteran was portrayed as a psychotic, drug-crazed killer. America was made to fear and despise the veteran and to blame him for the situation in Vietnam.

The Vietnam veterans were the children of the post-World War II 'baby boom.' We grew up at a time when the right and might of the United States was rarely if ever questioned. The Cold War and Dulles' 'Domino Theory' made us fear and despise Communist ideology. We were weaned on the World War II and post-World War II movie era and it had an effect on how we viewed war, the armed forces and our duty to fight for the 'American Way.' It made us feel invulnerable and worse still, it glorified war.

Unlike the average age of the American combat soldier in World War II of 26, the average age of Vietnam combat troops was only 19 years of age. And although the vast majority of us went to Vietnam because we really did believe in the war, we were boys not men. Unlike the propaganda of the movie image, Vietnam did not make us men, it disillusioned us.

The MacNamara 'big business approach' to war changed even the way we went to Vietnam. Instead of being recruited and sent as units, we were sent as individuals. Within thirty hours of leaving home we landed at an airfield in a war zone. All the basic training and drill did not prepare us adequately from the abrupt transition from peace to war. The United States as a nation was not at war. Only those who were sent to Vietnam were at war and the majority of them had been drafted. Once in Vietnam the arrivals were given individual assignments in the 'Vietnam war machine.' We were the 'newbies.' Just as we would eventually become the seasoned troops, the soldiers who received us looked on us sadly and did not really want to know us. We merely filled the slot and reminded them of someone who had been lucky enough to go home to his family, or unlucky enough to go home to a grave.

Once in our assigned niche not one month would pass before we recognized the absurdity of the situation. The movie image was shattered. For some the war was nothing more than sitting in a rear echelon area counting fatigues or turning a wrench on a vehicle. Others were catapulted into forward areas where they looked for booby traps at every step and eyed the LIPs (Local Indigenous Personnel) with distrust. The absurdity grew with American disengagement from the war. There were still front line combat units but the rear echelon grew larger. Medals were handed out for the most ridiculous reasons. Meritorious Service Medals were given to Brigade or Division Soldier of the Quarter – a troop who did his job, kept his fatigues pressed and his boots shined. By comparison in the later years of the war combat decorations for even the most courageous acts were rarely given to enlisted men, though officers often received them.

By late 1971 troops serving at MACV Headquarters in Saigon were required to wear Class B Dress Uniforms on weekends. Command headquarters throughout Vietnam were beginning to look like any other Army post in the United States, yet the war was still going on. On one occasion after returning from a ground mission I was refused admittance to a Corps Headquarters base because my dirty camouflaged fatigues were not the regulation dress on the base. As incidents multiplied the 'I don't give a damn' attitude was fed and nurtured by the situation in Vietnam and the welcome the veteran received when he returned.

The return of the combat veteran

from Vietnam had done more to affect and harm him than perhaps any other factor. Within 30 hours a combat veteran was taken from a war environment and returned to peace and normality. Although his family were usually there to greet him, homecoming was a terrible strain. There was a combined relief and guilt and, although the family was overjoyed, they were tentative in their approach. No one quite knew what to say, or what to leave unsaid. Outside the family there were non-veteran friends who tended to act as though he had only been away to college for a year.

There were more disabled veterans than ever before. The fatality rate in Vietnam was dramatically reduced by the helicopter, which allowed wounded soldiers to be within minutes of the most expert medical care. So the number of men left alive but disabled increased. The American prisoners of war aroused much concern and there was a great deal of happiness when they were released. Yet even after their ordeal, there were members of the government who would seek to punish them and lay guilt at their doors. In one instance the efforts of a politician to bring charges against a group of veterans for collaboration and treason caused many of the ex-prisoners at whom he pointed a finger to commit suicide.

It was only some eight years after the war ended that the experiences of the Vietnam combat soldier were recognized as having caused lingering and damaging effects. The problems of the combat veteran have been classified as the Vietnam veteran delayed stress syndrome. This is not an emotional or mental illness, but a normal function of the mind. It is a coping mechanism which enables a person to function during periods of extreme stress, when severe pain or death are threatened. The natural reactions are suppressed so that the person can continue to function. Without this mechanism the stress of the situation overwhelms the individual. The outcome of stress in such situations is the need of individuals to talk.

The important release of telling war stories and of sharing war experiences were generally denied to the Vietnam War veteran. Part of the problem was that on the flight back to the United States combat veterans were among men who were strangers to one another, although they had all experienced the war. Vietnam was actually the first war in which men did not have a significant interval among comrades between the war and home, during which they could relate their experiences. This ability to relate and discuss the feelings of stress situations is essential if the individual is to cope with the after effects. It was again denied the veteran when he returned to family and friends who had not experienced the war and so could not sympathize. The veteran was confused, out of place, and often struggling with guilt. The loneliness of the flight home and in family surroundings, combined with the anti-war atmosphere in the States, forced the combat veteran to bury his stress. This cannot be done without consequences and the consequences are at last being recognised.

Studies indicate that more than 60 percent of Vietnam combat veterans have some sort of delayed stress disorder and 40–60 percent have persistant emotional problems. Vietnam combat veterans have a higher divorce rate, a higher suicide rate and a higher criminal conviction rate than their civilian counterparts. One myth has also been dispelled. While there is a higher rate of alcoholism among veterans, the rate of drug addiction is dramatically lower than average. Delayed stress disorder is also evidenced by the fact that a large proportion of combat veterans only spend from eighteen months to two years in a job before they try something new.

Only now is the delayed stress syndrome being dealt with. Groups of specialists who are themselves Vietnam combat veterans are establishing 'vet centers' throughout the United States. They have recognized the problems and are urging combat veterans to join others and discuss their emotions and their difficulties and a high ratio of success is being achieved. The Veterans' Administration of the United States Government has always existed to help the veteran, and it does support the Vet Centers, but the unique problems of the Vietnam veteran were not sufficiently recognized.

Below: the nuclear-powered aircraft carrier USS Enterprise *is docked at Subic Bay in the Philippines before carrying the helicopters used in Operation Frequent Wind back to their base in Hawaii.*

The Balance Sheet

When one who has been personally involved in Vietnam attempts to draw conclusions about the war, old frustrations and 'wounds' creep to the forefront of any discussion. The passions and emotions of anyone who was personally affected by the war are mingled with personal truths and bias. What was so different about Vietnam? Why did it last so long? Why did it throw the United States into turmoil and divide the generations to such an extent that it almost seemed as if America were on the brink of civil war? Most important, why after all the lives, time, money, and military expertise that were invested into the countries of South Vietnam, Laos, and Cambodia did they fall? Why did the Communists ultimately win the war?

One of the answers to these questions rests with the fact that America failed to establish a stable, non-Communist South Vietnam. Regardless of the promises that were made by the numerous governments of South Vietnam that they would continue to fight against the Communists, the country on the whole never achieved stability. The Vietnamese people never felt secure, nor saw any reason to fight for their government. The United States entered the war knowing this situation. Particularly during the Vietnamization program the winning of the hearts and minds of the people of South Vietnam was never pursued with the same fervour as the efforts to kill the enemy. The military effort came first and the people and their problems were pushed down the list of priorities.

This is not to say that American values are misguided, but the pursuit of those values in Vietnam was misdirected. America went to South Vietnam to fight the Communist, rather than to aid the people as a whole. The task of supporting and stabilizing the lives of the Vietnamese people was left to the government of South Vietnam and, although millions of dollars were sent to that government, the United States turned a blind eye to the corruption and greed that syphoned that money away.

The Vietnamese people saw the Americans as perpetrators of the suffering which the war had brought; unsympathetic to their needs and problems and more often than not exploiting them. The American soldiers did not want to know the Vietnamese, but wanted only to use them for menial labor, self-gratification, and often as scapegoats for the frustrations and anger they felt against the enemy and the war. America gave them nothing and expected loyalty in return. The Vietnamese people saw only one side of the American people and the United States and most often it was the worst side.

It was this mistrust, misunderstanding, callousness and even hatred between the people, the government, and the Americans which ultimately led to the fall of South Vietnam. But this alone is not sufficient explanation of the sudden collapse of South Vietnam in 1975. That collapse can be attributed to more specific factors. The loss of United States military support, particularly in the areas of air power, artillery and communications obviously weakened the South. When American forces left Vietnam in 1973 the elaborate systems which had been established were either removed by the Americans or fell into disuse and disrepair. South Vietnamese pilots feared enemy antiaircraft fire and refused to conduct ground attack missions at low level. The ARVN high command had problems in identifying targets against which artillery fire would do the most damage. Americans had performed these tasks and the loss of their support and guidance meant that field officers were left to fend for themselves.

Another important factor was the corruption and indecisiveness of the South Vietnamese government. Government officials spent much of their time and aid money on personal pleasures and very little of either on government duties and programs. That attitude was apparent from the President of the Republic down to the lowliest official. Black market activities were at their peak during Thieu's government, with military supplies and other much needed commodities being sold by government officials for high profit. High positions in the government went to the highest bidder and corruption was rife in both government and armed forces, no matter what the long term damage might be.

The South Vietnamese Government believed that the United States would continue to provide military assistance even after the Paris Peace Agreement of 1973. The Vietnamese could not believe that America wanted nothing more to do with Vietnam, but after the passage of the American Presidential War Powers Act in 1973 little could be done without Congressional approval. Such approval would be difficult to obtain, due to the public feelings about Vietnam and war in general.

The South Vietnamese suffered the depressing effects of the United States withdrawal. They could not understand that, after all the American expenditure of time, money, and lives, the United States could regard Vietnam as no longer important. The

United States' Vietnamization program had not done enough to develop leadership or to instill a sense of self-reliance in the ARVN ranks. The program had begun late and the Americans had left before it became fully effective. The ARVN soldier was like a child when compared to the enemy. He had become accustomed to heavy air and artillery support and had relied on American vehicles and helicopters. The United States had shouldered too great a share of the war and when the ARVN had to fight for their lives in 1975 they could not.

South Vietnam was 'boxed-in' strategically. When the Communists were finally prepared to launch the last offensive, South Vietnam had its back to the wall. It was surrounded by Communist governments on all borders and its only allies had withdrawn. Thieu's 'no retreat' orders in the final days gave no leeway to the army and the majority of the troops believed they were being needlessly sacrificed without hope of victory.

Above: the emblem of the Vietnam Veterans Against the War.
Left: a Marine guard keeps a close watch on the South Vietnamese refugees evacuated from Saigon, as they line up on USS Hancock's flight deck. Operation Frequent Wind marked the end of the United State's military involvement in the Vietnam conflict.

Through the ineptitude of the government, troops were rushed about the country without realizing what was happening, or what strategy could be used against the invaders.

Finally, the emotions of the people played a part. They suddenly realized that the United States was not coming to their aid and that realization destroyed their will to resist. The people and the army of South Vietnam may not have had a great love for the Americans, but they had grown used to the Americans coming to their aid.

The last question that must be answered is whether Vietnam was worth the cost. America had invested more than 150,000,000,000 dollars in the war. More than 50,000 Americans were dead and 200,000 wounded. The United States had torn itself apart over the war. Demonstrations and especially the Kent State riots, had caused deep wounds. The United States had lost support throughout the world and in some circles old friends and allies were driven away as the war continued.

The United States entered the conflict to demonstrate her determination to fight Communist expansion. This policy was instituted in the Truman and Eisenhower years and compounded by Kennedy's injured pride. Johnson continued the war, as did Nixon for a time, because neither wanted to be known as the President who had allowed the Communists to take Southeast Asia. Nixon saw a way out, but wanted South Vietnam to seem secure for a time so that any peace made by his Administration did not appear as a betrayal. The American people indicated that they had had enough of the war and Nixon used their decision as his means of escape from a hopeless situation.

The people of South Vietnam wanted only to carry on their lives without fear, but with the arrival of United States forces, they were no longer able to maintain their way of life. They became a people living on handouts. A war to fight oppression is a noble war, but the lack of concern for the people of South Vietnam was an oppression in itself.

Vietnam thrust the United States into a period of indecisiveness and growing weakness in its foreign policies. It broke the will of the American people to fight for a just cause, which is only now in the 1980s being revived. The only possible value of Vietnam are the lessons to be learned and pondered by future American policy-makers. Never assume that you can fight a coalition war and successfully reform your ally at the same time. Do not expect support from other countries, no matter how idealistic the war may be. Do not try to reshape your ally and its army in your own image. Do not count on technology or on sophisticated weaponry to assure victory. The learning of these fundamental lessons has cost America dear, but if the lessons have been truly learned and the mistakes are not repeated then perhaps it was not all in vain.

The Vietnam War was a violent era in American history on which much will eventually be written. A final understanding will only be reached when attempts to fix the blame, against the Government, the military, the people, and the media can be set aside. Perhaps understanding will only come when all those who have lived through the experience are dead and the facts can be assessed more objectively. It will be at least a generation before 'Vietnam' will mean anything but a war of agony, frustration, and humiliation.

Index

Page numbers in italics refer to illustrations.

Picture Credits
Author's Collection: p 189.
Bison Picture Library: pp 13 (lower), 16, 17, 18 (lower), 19 (right), 20–21, 101 (upper), 144, 157 (upper), 160 (lower), 161, 172, 173, 177, 180–181.
Richard Natkiel: pp 14 (upper), 103, 171 (upper).
USAF: pp 54, 55, 59, 94 (lower), 96 (lower), 102, 106 (lower), 107, 110–111, 130–131, 134, 135, 138–139, 142–143, 146–147, 150–151, 154–155, 158–159, 162–163, 166–167, 170, 171 (lower).
US Army: pp 8–9, 10, 11, 14 (lower), 15, 18 (upper), 19 (left), 22, 24–25, 26, 27, 28, 32, 33, 34, 35, 36, 37, 38, 39, 40, 41, 42, 43, 44, 45, 46, 47, 48, 50, 51, 52, 53, 56–57, 58, 60, 61, 62–63, 64, 65, 66, 67, 68–69, 70 (lower), 71, 72–73, 74–75, 76–77, 78–79, 80–81, 82 (upper), 84–85, 86–87, 89, 91 (lower), 92–93, 94 (upper), 95, 98, 99, 100, 101 (lower), 104–105, 106 (upper), 108, 109, 112 (left), 113, 114–115, 116–117, 118–119, 120–121, 122, 123, 124, 125, 126–127, 128, 129, 132–133, 134, 136, 137, 140, 148–149, 152, 153, 156, 157 (lower), 160 (upper), 168–169, 174–175.
US Marines: pp 70 (upper), 82 (lower), 112 (right), 176, 178–179, 182, 184, 185, 186–187, 188–189.
US Navy: pp 12, 13 (upper), 23, 29, 88, 90, 91 (upper), 96 (lower), 97, 145, 164–165.